By All Means

Baker James Cauthen
and Others

CONVENTION PRESS
Nashville Tennessee

A publication of the
FOREIGN MISSION BOARD
Richmond, Virginia

572-43071

Library of Congress Catalog Card Number: 59-9679

Printed in the United States of America

115.D58C.

Preface

"I AM made all things to all men, that I might BY ALL MEANS save some," the apostle Paul said in his first letter to the Corinthians (9:22).

This book, *By All Means,* is an account of the various missionary "means" or methods used by Southern Baptists in lands beyond their own. It was written by the Foreign Mission Board's six secretaries. All of the authors are ordained ministers who have served in the pastorate. Most of them have served theological seminaries as missions professors.

Baker J. Cauthen, who wrote the first chapter, is the Board's executive secretary and a former missionary to China.

Winston Crawley, who wrote the second chapter, is secretary for the Orient and a former missionary to the Philippines.

Frank K. Means, author of the third chapter, is secretary for Latin America.

H. Cornell Goerner, who wrote the fourth chapter, is secretary for Africa, Europe, and the Near East.

Eugene L. Hill, coauthor of the fifth chapter, is

secretary for missionary education and promotion and a former missionary to China and Malaya.

Elmer S. West, second author for the final chapter, is secretary for missionary personnel.

GENEVIEVE GREER
Book Editor
Foreign Mission Board

Contents

1

World Evangelism Today

IT is a moving experience to visit the Carey Baptist Church in Calcutta, India, and to see there the baptistry in which, on September 6, 1812, William Ward, an English Baptist missionary associated with William Carey, baptized Adoniram Judson and his wife, Ann Hasseltine. The Judsons had left America the preceding February as Congregational missionaries. On the long sea voyage, study of the New Testament concerning baptism convinced them of the rightness of the Baptist position. Upon being baptized, they resigned from the Congregational mission and wrote letters to Baptists in America, offering themselves as their missionary representatives should Baptists see fit to organize for their support.

Standing in that church in Calcutta, one can visualize the difficulties that confronted the young couple. They were thousands of miles from home with no assurance of support from any source. The British East India Company, then in power in India, was unfriendly toward their efforts and forced them to leave the country. They settled in Burma in 1813, and many trials awaited them there. The story of Judson's imprisonment, during which the tender love and care of Ann Hasseltine constantly supported him, is one of the most beautiful in the annals of Christian history. By the time Judson's work came to a close on April 12, 1850, the mission in Burma was firmly established.

Hundreds of heroic missionary lives have been invested in the service of Christ in many lands. Many of those lives are well known to Christian people. Others are like stars that can only be seen faintly.

The heroism involved in missionary dedication is not something that belongs only to the early days of missions. Those who are privileged to attend meetings of the Foreign Mission Board are constantly blessed by the testimonies of men and women who turn aside from challenging opportunities at the home base to follow Christ across the world.

Some of the most heroic examples of devotion in the history of Christian missions have been written during the last twenty years. Servants of God in war-torn countries have worked amid uncertainty and danger. Many of them have lost their possessions, and some have endured weary months in a concentration camp, and yet have found joy in suffering with Christ. Families have been divided, yet have carried on their service for the Lord with radiant faith. Some missionaries, even in these days, have been called upon to give their lives in martyrdom.

Viewing this complete dedication of life, one cannot escape the question, "What is the basic purpose of world missions?" The question can be asked in another way: "What are these people undertaking to do as they go across the world?"

PURPOSE OF MISSIONS

Every missionary would say that his basic purpose is to share the gospel of redemption with a world that needs to know. Every missionary has been stirred by the words of Jesus, "Go ye, therefore, and make disciples."

The missionary is an evangelist. He is one who communicates the gospel of redemption. He can never stop with simply making it known, but yearns over the people to whom he goes, and prays for God's power that those who hear may know a living Saviour. It is a joy to the missionary to proclaim the gospel of life, but his joy is incomplete until he sees people trust Christ as personal Saviour and experience the touch of his transforming grace upon their lives.

Communicating the gospel of redemption, however, is not the whole purpose of world missions. Every missionary regards his task as being that of bringing the people who accept Christ into the fellowship of New Testament churches.

This mission concept calls for great emphasis upon the establishment and development of churches. These churches must follow the New Testament pattern. They must spring out of the life of regenerated men and women in fellowship with their living Lord.

Christ never remains a foreigner in any land. People who come to know him feel their oneness with their Saviour and think of him as being very near. The Bible never seems to be a foreign book. People who read the New Testament love it as if it had been written directly for them. In many instances, their cultures enable them to understand parts of it even more readily than we do in our western civilization. Since Christ is so thoroughly identified with the people of each land, and since the Bible is a book that makes its home among every people, the churches that come into life achieve their best ministries by becoming truly indigenous.

Churches must never become foreign institutions to which people are invited. The people must feel that the churches are their own, under the leadership of Christ. New Testament churches on mission fields, as at the home base, are self-governing. Approximately two thirds of the organized churches on mission fields are self-supporting. As early as possible they secure pastors from among their own countrymen. Music is adapted to their own background, and as time goes on, hymns are written to express their own experience with Christ.

A missionary does not conceive of his purpose simply in terms of establishing indigenous churches. Those churches must be centers of evangelism. Until a church is convinced of its distinctive ministry of evangelism, it has not become thoroughly established.

There is a tendency for non-Christian religions to erect temples in choice places and await the coming of those who wish to seek what may be found there. Christians sense the imperative of Christ to take his message to the people. Christians must be seekers. They must not wait to be sought.

The hope of the world lies not in the control of the world's affairs by churches. Indeed, the tragedy and decay that accompany such a trend have been adequately demonstrated in the past. Hope lies in leading people to know Christ as Saviour and to follow him as Lord in every aspect of life. Dynamic Christians in every phase of the world's affairs could bring a new day. The attainment of this hope calls for the establishing of churches that are committed to the evangelization of the world.

People who do not know Christ seldom understand what can motivate Christians to lay hand to such a purpose as has been described. Some consider it an interference with the lives and cultures of people in other lands. Some regard it as overzealous enthusiasm. Others regard it as an inexplainable phenomenon.

When a person knows Christ as Saviour and saturates his heart with the teachings of the Bible, life looks different. He becomes aware of the world in which he lives, and he shares the compassion of Jesus. He becomes conscious of an amazing degree of physical and social need in the world, and cannot remain indifferent to human distress. As he reads the story of the good Samaritan, it makes him eager to do all he can to heal the sick, comfort the sad, feed the hungry, educate the illiterate, and provide for the homeless.

He sees, too, a need far deeper than that which

greets the eye. He recognizes that man's basic want is spiritual. Even in countries where no great amount of poverty, illiteracy, and human misery are found, there is profound spiritual illness. This is a world of sin-sick humanity desperately in need of the Saviour.

As the Christian becomes aware of man's need, he also recognizes the Master's mandate. To find and do the will of Christ becomes for him the highest privilege. He understands that just as Jesus grew in obedience to the will of his Heavenly Father, so every Christian must grow in obedience to the divine will. When he recognizes the clear command of Christ as given in the Great Commission, a sense of responsibility lies upon his heart.

A missionary is motivated by love for his Lord and for his fellow man. Aware of the abundance of grace that he has received, he wants his life to express his gratitude and love toward his Lord, from whom he has received it. Recognizing sin in himself, and conscious that there is even more of it than he sees, he is constantly reminded of the wonder of Christ's love. In return, he has a growing love for his Lord. This love causes him to want to follow the will of his Master.

The love of Christ in a man's heart causes him to love his fellow man. He desires that all men might know Christ and longs to relieve their distresses. The motivation of love causes him to go beyond the normal extent of his duty and leads him to serve in the spirit of the Cross.

THE PATTERN

As a missionary undertakes the task of evangelism, he is guided by the pattern laid down in the New Testament. This pattern may be seen in the ministry of Jesus, in the Great Commission, in the history recorded in the Acts of the Apostles, and in statements made in the Epistles. Volumes might be written about what the missionary can learn from the New Testament concerning evangelism. Only a few suggestions can be given here.

In the ministry of Jesus the missionary cannot but see the power of personal influence. It is evident in the accounts of Jesus' life that people were greatly impressed by what Jesus was in himself. His personal relationship with God, the vitality of his prayer life, the calm and poise of his heart, the depth of his convictions, and his clear insight into truth made an impact upon all who came in touch with him. Even his bitterest enemies who sought to lay hands upon him bore testimony, "Never man spake like this man."

As he looks upon the ministry of his Lord, a missionary must conclude that on a mission field his greatest service will consist of reflecting the spirit and love of Christ in his personal life. The radiance of a devoted Christian life, in a land where the gospel is little known, is hard to overstate.

Because so much is dependent upon the quality of his life, each missionary must give the most careful attention to his relationship to his Lord.

From the ministry of Jesus, the missionary also observes the high value to be placed upon preaching and teaching the Word of God. He observes that every experience can become an opportunity for witnessing to the truth, and is impressed with the way in which this witness is to be borne.

The simple manner in which Jesus stated profound truth is a great example for the missionary. His use of illustrations from everyday life and his employment of language that was understood readily by the people, encourage the missionary as he struggles for mastery of a foreign language.

The note of authority with which Jesus spoke was so characteristic of his teaching that the missionary is impressed with the fact that, if he refrains from his own ideas and conveys faithfully the word of his Lord, his message will come to the hearers with the same note of authority.

From the ministry of Jesus, the missionary learns compassion for human suffering. Wherever our Master was surrounded by the sick and sorrowing, his heart overflowed in love and mercy. His wonderful acts of healing were expressions of his loving heart and clear demonstrations of the truth.

From the ministry of Jesus, a missionary learns breadth of interest and concern. Our Master was as eager to help the rich taxgatherer in Jericho as to help the blind beggar by the wayside; he was as much at home in the house of the wealthy as in the humblest surroundings. The missionary must remember that the gospel is for all people and not for one segment of it.

Every missionary is impressed with Jesus' training of his twelve chosen followers. Our Master did not measure his achievement in terms of the numbers who came to hear him. He was not overelated because great masses thronged upon him; on the contrary, he warned his disciples of the days of rejection that he knew would come. He was not overwhelmed with discouragement when multitudes turned away. He laid stress upon training individuals whose hearts had been opened, and he prepared them to continue with their witness after his departure.

Missionaries recognize the importance of preparing faithful workers to bear the gospel message and to give leadership to emerging Christian work. While the missionary rejoices in every individual he wins to Christ personally, he does not measure the impact of his ministry merely in those terms. He sees a chain reaction as trained individuals in turn reach others for their Lord.

The New Testament pattern of evangelism is indicated in the familiar words of the Great Commission. Because his Lord said, "All authority in heaven and on earth has been given to me," the missionary undertakes his task knowing that he is properly authorized to do so. Nothing is more reassuring than to know that one is in his place of responsibility by the mandate of his Master. The task the missionary has undertaken is not of human origin; it is commanded by the sovereign Lord of heaven and earth. Amid all discouragements, and in the face of any opposition, God's servant is encouraged by remembering that he has undertaken his labor upon the authority of his Lord.

In the Great Commission it is clearly stated that we are to go and "make disciples." The missionary keeps in mind that his going is not in itself a fulfilment of his Lord's will. He keeps in mind that merely proclaiming the truth is not a fulfilment of his Lord's will. He remembers that he is to "make disciples." This calls upon him so to live, pray, and use all means of Christian witness, as to help people accept Christ as Saviour and Lord. The missionary is thrown back upon dependence on the Holy Spirit to open the hearts of those about him.

He remembers that the Great Commission commands us to go to "all nations." In the hardest fields, where gains are slow, he is encouraged by remembering that the commission applies to those difficult places. Our Lord does not command us to go on a vain mission. The gospel is the power of God unto salvation to every person who believes, and there is no area in the world where the hearts of men cannot be opened by the Holy Spirit. We are particularly impressed by this fact as we consider the limited Christian witness in the Moslem world. We have a heavy burden upon our hearts as we remember how limited has been our own witness among millions of Moslems, and reflect that perhaps we have not done more because the work is so difficult.

In the Great Commission we find that we are to baptize those who believe, and to teach them to observe all that our Lord has commanded. This underscores the importance of establishing churches and nurturing them in the work of the Lord. Everything that is done in the growing of New Testament churches at the home base needs to be done on mission fields. The work of the missionary is largely devoted to developing churches.

In the Great Commission our Lord stated, "And, lo, I am with you alway, even unto the end of the world." A missionary relies upon this encouragement. He knows that in all circumstances he has the companionship of his Saviour and does not need to depend upon his own strength. He is assured that in time the Word of God will bear fruit.

The pattern of New Testament evangelism is also disclosed in the Acts of the Apostles. The dominant figure there is our Lord himself, working through his Holy Spirit in the lives of his messengers. The same Lord who walked through Galilee and personally taught his disciples is still in their midst. They feel his presence and are aware of his power. The missionary goes to his task of world evangelism convinced that the Lord Jesus lives today just as he did in the days of the apostles.

The Acts of the Apostles reveals the strategy used in world evangelization. On the one hand, there was a wide dispersion of the gospel; on the other hand, there was concentration.

Even in the limited years covered by the book of Acts, the gospel of Christ was taken over a vast area of the world. One of the greatest hindrances to world evangelism lies in the point of view that says there should be no wide dispersion of laborers and effort, but rather a concentration in a few limited places. Even missionaries must be on guard lest they fall into a pattern of concentrating in one place and neglecting broad areas of need beyond it. We should be challenged constantly by the blank places on our world mission map, showing where we need to expand our testimony.

As we look at this New Testament strategy, we are impressed that there is concentration as well as wide deployment of Christian witness. The apostle Paul spent much time in Antioch, Corinth, Ephesus, and Rome, where churches had been established. There must be wide dispersion in order that witness can be borne; but it is necessary that there be concentration in order that strong centers may be developed and the fruit of the gospel be preserved.

In the days of the apostles, work was established in large cities and from there was projected into surrounding areas. One of the remarkable features of our present day is the growth of great cities across the world. We are living in a time when worldwide industrialization promotes the growth of cities. The countries of the Orient are undergoing a vast industrial revolution, and the largest cities in the world undoubtedly will be found in the Orient in a few years. Tokyo, Japan, already stands in the first rank of the world's major cities.

A strategy of world evangelism calls for establishing in the cities great centers of influence from which large surrounding areas may be evangelized. In many major cities the growth of large universities provides opportunity for influencing those who will be leaders in their nations.

Paul's ministry in Ephesus gives evidence of what can be done under the power of God's Holy Spirit in a great metropolitan center. When a city experiences a mighty spiritual movement, the impact is widely felt.

We must face the task of world evangelism in our day with fresh plans for evangelistic efforts in the main cities of the world. In that way the tempo of Christian witness can be greatly accelerated.

In the Acts of the Apostles we observe that the crises which come to nations can turn out for the furtherance of the gospel. When the people were scattered abroad from Jerusalem, following the death of Stephen, the gospel was scattered over a wide area.

The tragic occurrences in China, the oldest mission field of Southern Baptists, have become the occasion of missionary advance in the Orient. In the days of war with Japan, our missionary work in China was reduced to a skeleton staff, with as few as fifteen missionaries there at one time. It was during this emergency that our work was projected into Hawaii and strengthened in Latin America and Africa.

With the rise of communism, missionaries were forced out of China. By the end of 1951 not one Southern Baptist missionary remained there. Two observations grew out of those tragic occurrences. We note that the emergency became the occasion of a wide spread of the gospel in other lands, and we are today more widely extended in mission work in the Far East than ever before in our history. This development probably would not have come about had there been no crisis in China. We also observe that even amid emergencies and without missionary assistance, the work of the Lord goes on when once it is established.

Conditions in China are tragic. Many Christian leaders are in prison there. Many churches have been forced to close. Ministers and other Christians are constantly in peril. Amid all this, however, Christian work keeps going forward. We are convinced that the gospel of Christ in China has been firmly planted, and will outlive the Communist regime.

We learn from the book of Acts the value of concentrating missionary effort on the development of local churches. The true measure of any missionary undertaking must be determined in terms of church development. It is possible to establish extensive institutions and have weak church development. Whenever great institutions are established, but minor attention is given to the growth of New Testament churches, the work is basically weak. In times of emergency those institutions can be closed or brought under such control of government that their Christian witness is paralyzed; but strong churches survive.

The basic policy of the Foreign Mission Board is to send forth missionaries who will lead people to Christ and bring them into the fellowship of New Testament churches that project, through their associations and conventions, programs of ministry as led by the Holy Spirit.

It is instructive to note in the book of Acts that the servants of God are leaders but not rulers of the churches. Missionaries wisely consider themselves to be servants of the churches that have been established. They are teachers and leaders but are not rulers. The purpose of the missionary is to assist in the development of strong, autonomous churches, having national pastors and functioning with a consciousness of responsibility to Christ. Churches across the world are not held in tutelage by missionaries nor controlled by the Foreign Mission Board. They are planted upon the principle of being sovereign New Testament churches responsible to their Lord, working co-operatively with their fellow churches.

The New Testament pattern of evangelism is indicated also in the Epistles of the New Testament. Space does not permit full discussion of these principles, but a few can be mentioned.

For one thing, it is evident in the Epistles that major emphasis must be placed on thorough instruction of the churches in Christian truth. A reading of Galatians indicates the importance of this as seen by the apostle Paul. The missionary must be careful that the gospel is understood and that Christian teaching is faithfully imparted.

This is particularly true in Baptist life, because the only control over a Baptist church is that which is exerted by the truth itself. Unless churches are properly indoctrinated in the Word of God, they can be swept away by heretical teaching and their witness paralyzed.

A study of the Epistles also indicates the importance to be given to the spiritual life of the churches. In most instances, as the apostles wrote letters to the churches they devoted part of the letter to a statement of Christian principles and part to application of those principles to daily living. It is imperative that Christian truth always be vitally related to personal conduct. The missionary does not go to launch a reforming movement. When, however, he presents Christian truth properly and applies it to human living, it becomes the greatest reforming force in the world. Wherever the gospel goes, the life of the people is changed.

A study of the Epistles also indicates that attention must be given to organization of churches. The pattern for church organization that will apply to any mission field is clearly indicated in the New Testament. Pastors and deacons are needed, and the church must function in a self-governing manner. High qualities of Christian character must control those who lead in the work of the churches.

The Epistles also point up the value of stewardship. The letters of the apostle Paul indicate that he called upon people in poverty and deep need to share with others and support the work of their churches.

On mission fields, the development of good stewards is especially important. This must come about in order that Christians may express their love for their Lord. It must be the response of compassion toward the needy. It must be a sharing in the labor of Christ by providing for the needs of the church. At times it seems difficult to call upon poor people to give, yet it is important that they give in order that their Christian lives may develop.

As work develops on foreign mission fields, the strategy is to give assistance as need arises. The Foreign Mission Board does not design what should be done by Baptists in other lands, but rather awaits the moving of God's Spirit upon those New Testament churches as they work together in their associations and conventions. As they sense the leadership of their sovereign Lord and request assistance to enable them to do that which is beyond their own strength, it gives joy to the Foreign Mission Board to channel the missionary resources of Southern Baptists to their help.

It should be understood that the Southern Baptist missionary enterprise is not a movement whereby we go into foreign countries to establish ourselves and direct people to do according to our bidding. It is, rather, a movement of sharing, whereby we go into countries to make known the living Lord and to work with the churches that emerge as the people follow Christ.

On this basis we are colaborers with the Baptists of Japan, Brazil, Nigeria, and other lands throughout the world, as they, with their fully independent churches and autonomous Baptist conventions, project under the leadership of Christ those ministries that they believe to be pleasing to their Master. This does not paralyze action. Rather, we think and share together, and the Spirit of God leads on into a constant expansion of the witness begun in his name.

OUR WORLD

In thinking of evangelism, it is necessary that we consider the world situation as it relates to our Christian task.

Upon looking at the map, we note vast areas that are closed to missionary service. China has historically been our largest mission field, but we have no missionaries serving there now, and no money can be sent there to reinforce Christian work. The advance of communism into any land means the termination of missionary opportunity there. It inevitably brings severe limitations upon Christian work. As we consider the areas closed to missionary service, we are confronted with a remarkable challenge to intercessory prayer.

Closed areas serve as reminders that lands now open may become closed. We are called to action while there is opportunity. We must use wise strategy so that the work planted in every area may be able to continue even if conditions should force the withdrawal of missionaries.

Our day is frequently described in terms of world revolution. This does not mean that communism has produced a world revolution. It means that rising levels of literacy and development of industry throughout the world have created an awareness of the great possibilities of the average man. They have also brought into sharp focus the heavy burden of misery and human distress that millions of people endure.

A spirit of revolt has arisen in the hearts of the world's people against the circumstances under which they must live and die. Worldwide demand for a decent way of life is growing out of a common conviction that it is not necessary for human beings to pass through their earthly existence in poverty, illiteracy, and privation.

As industrialization makes rapid strides in undeveloped parts of the world, this world revolution will be accentuated. Developments in radio, newspapers, motion pictures, and world travel will increase its pace. Communism undertakes to seize this world unrest for its own ends. It declares itself the champion of the needy man and describes communism as the answer to the world's need.

Another feature of our day is an awakening spirit of nationalism throughout every part of the world.

Many Oriental nations that formerly were held in colonial status have attained independence. The Western world is realizing the significance of a reawakened Oriental nationalism. Many are realizing that China and India have had ancient cultures and have been mighty powers.

Nationalism has reached new heights throughout Latin America. The United States wisely is emphasizing a "good neighbor" policy.

New nations are being born throughout Africa. That continent long has been an area of colonialism, but the situation is changing. The emergence of Ghana and Nigeria as self-governing countries has brought a new day. Many people feel that it is only a matter of time until the colonial era in Africa will have passed entirely.

The Near East in recent years has evidenced determination to throw off all remnants of colonialism. Memory of the past glories of their own ancient empires dwells in the minds of those people.

This intensive nationalism creates difficulties for mission work in many instances. It creates problems in securing permission for missionaries to live in some lands. It causes nationals to be sensitive about their own prerogatives and their national pride.

Every missionary does well to consider himself a guest in the country to which he goes. He should not regard himself as being there with priority rights and privileges because he is an American citizen. Remembering that he is there by permission of the host country, he should relate himself to the nationals as he would expect foreigners to relate themselves to the citizens of his own land.

Closely allied with awakening nationalism is a renascence of ancient religions. Our day is characterized by a religious stirring throughout the whole world. There is a notable religious awakening in the Orient.

At the close of the second World War, Japan presented an extraordinary opportunity for Christian missions. The spiritual needs of the people were so great that their hunger could not wait on the slow efforts that were made. Many Buddhist and Shinto sects sprang up in Japan, along with other religious organizations that can be classified neither as Buddhist nor Shinto.

Buddhism has experienced an awakening throughout the Orient. Its leaders have spent many months in consultation, considering the modern world in the light of their Buddhist beliefs.

In countries like Thailand and Malaya, the influence of Buddhism is particularly strong. In Thailand it is the established religion, protected by the government. Temples abound everywhere, and every man enters the priesthood for a period in his life. It is very difficult there for a person to break with Buddhism and follow Christ.

There is marked religious renascence in India also. Hinduism has been so linked with Indian nationalism that many people regard a breach with that religion as a departure from India's national heritage.

Vast emphasis is placed upon Islam as vital to national aspirations in the Moslem world. Islam seeks not only to strengthen its hold on the lands where it now is in power, but its leaders have laid far-reaching plans for its spread.

In view of the combination of intensified nationalism and reviving ancient religions, it is obvious that the task of world evangelism is becoming more difficult.

Reference has already been made to the challenge of world communism. This ideology which scorns all religion is actually a religion in itself. Establishing the state in the position that should be occupied only by God, it demands of the individual a total surrender. The loyalties which result from its totalitarian approach are sometimes most remarkable. The sacrifices and sufferings to which advocates of this movement submit to attain its purposes are amazing.

Communism regards itself as the answer to the world's need. It expects a dictatorship of the laboring class to bring in a new world order. Its fallacy lies at the point of eliminating the idea of God and thereby destroying the true meaning of human personality. A human being no longer is regarded as an individual with inherent rights, but is reduced to a unit of production.

One of the terrible dangers of communism is that it does not await popular approval in order to assume power. It merely requires that a set of circumstances prevail in which a well-organized Communist minority can seize the government and coerce the masses to do its will. The power of the movement to regiment whole populations is astounding. Merciless measures are used. By the ever-present hand of the secret police, the pattern of life under Communist control is entirely reshaped.

World evangelization faces in communism a major adversary. We do well to remember that communism is not static. It reaches into every country and works among all classes of people. Christianity cannot expect communism to desist from its propagating efforts. A new thrust of world evangelism must exceed all that the Communists undertake to do.

Another feature of the world today is a fantastic growth in population. This has been brought about by reduction of infant mortality, extension of the human life span, elimination of many of the dread diseases that have plagued mankind, and a lifting of standards of living. This growth does not seem of any great danger in our own country, but throughout the Far East the pressure of humanity upon the soil is already intense. In a few years China will have one billion people, and the other countries of the Far East will also be even more congested than they are today.

Amid this population increase, we need to be aware that the whole world is sensitive about all questions concerning race. Race is considered in some areas to be a matter of relationship between black and white people. Race relationships, however, are far more extensive. The racial background of nations of the Orient, where live half the world's population, is different from that of the West. Likewise, the nations of the Middle East are of a different racial group. The nations of Latin America have so adjusted themselves to racial groupings within their own midst that their point of view identifies them with the nonwhite peoples of the earth.

The nations are vitally concerned about what democracy has to offer the nonwhite world. They are not prepared to accept a democracy that calls for domination of one race over another because of the color of skin.

Most of the mission work projected by Southern

Baptists is among nonwhite peoples or among peoples whose point of view identifies them with the nonwhite races.

The delicate problems of racial relationships can be solved as people are brought into fellowship with Christ and with one another in love. The task of world evangelism in our day faces a real challenge at the point of race, and it should be borne in mind that every constructive attitude toward race at the home base reinforces the labor of world missions.

A NEW THRUST

In view of these factors that confront us, we are impressed with the imperative of Christian action now. The Christian movement has penetrated widespread areas of the world, but it has been a mere penetration.

One may put pins on a world map to indicate where missionaries are located and come to the erroneous conclusion that most fields have been occupied. The pin in the map may represent a city with a million people in which only a handful of Christian witnesses hold aloft the banner of Christ. Surrounding the city are vast rural areas in which there are villages and towns containing thousands of people who have never heard the message of salvation, and have merely heard the name of Christ with no understanding of its meaning.

Only a small fraction of the populations of these countries is Christian. One is overwhelmed by a sense of urgency as he remembers the amazing population explosion of our day. Percentagewise, the world is becoming more non-Christian every year. The increase of population outruns our total Christian effort.

We come to the inescapable conclusion that in our day the work of world evangelization must be greatly accelerated. What we have done in days gone by, commendable and worthy as it may be, is not sufficient for the day in which we live. The time has come when world evangelization must move forward with a new thrust.

This new thrust obviously calls for a greatly expanded missionary undertaking. We can interpret the resources which God is entrusting to Southern Baptists only in terms of his expectation of a greater worldwide witness. We have talked for several years in terms of a foreign mission staff of two thousand missionaries. This, however, is only the beginning. Southern Baptists should have had two thousand missionaries long ago. When we have attained that figure, it will be only a first step toward our Lord's objective.

It is also obvious that mission work must be expanded in every country where we are serving. In no case have we really occupied those lands. In Brazil, Nigeria, and Japan, lands where our greatest concentrations of missionaries are found, the needs for greatly enlarged missionary service are overwhelming.

Many countries into which we have never gone stand before us as a rebuke and a challenge. We are rebuked because we should have gone there long ago. We are challenged to enter without any more delay.

A forward thrust in world evangelism does not consist simply in placing more missionaries in more locations with more equipment to use in their work. It is a matter of stepping up the impact of our Christian witness throughout the world.

In accelerating this impact there are some guiding convictions which have been well tested. For one thing, it has been adequately shown that every New Testament principle of evangelism and church development which has blessed our work at the home base can be applied across the world.

As principles are applied in different places, new insight comes, and we find new ways to apply those principles more effectively.

The church is not a Western institution. It does not depend upon Western culture and thought patterns for its power of operation. A New Testament church is just as effective in Japan, or Nigeria, or Indonesia as it is in America or in Britain.

The growth which we have experienced in Southern Baptist life has not come by accident. Certain principles have been discovered and applied. The preaching of the gospel has continued in its simplicity and in fidelity to the Scriptures. The power of the Holy Spirit has been sought in prayer and faith. God would have us not only send money and missionaries, but share the principles of growth that have blessed every aspect of church life.

It is vital to keep in mind that we must work

through the emerging churches, associations, and conventions across the world. To disregard the initiative of the churches would be a major mistake.

It has been demonstrated that evangelism can be conducted throughout the world on a much greater scale. City-wide crusades, preaching missions, and simultaneous evangelistic efforts have been projected already in the Orient, Latin America, and Africa. It has been clearly demonstrated that these approaches to evangelism are sound and are productive.

We look forward to the time when large-scale evangelistic crusades will be an annual occurrence in the major cities of the world. The Foreign Mission Board annually sets aside money to be used for advance projects in evangelism and church development. These projects are undertaken upon the recommendation and request of the Baptist organizations on mission fields.

New modes of transportation make possible a new strategy never before used in world evangelism. Until a few years ago it was not possible to cross the world in a matter of hours. By means of air transportation, the most distant spot in the world is only a few hours away today. The time has come when the home base can share directly in the task of world evangelism.

This does not mean that the task of world evangelism can be done from the home base without sending out greatly increased numbers of missionaries. Such an approach would be as unrealistic as undertaking to grow a New Testament church by having periodic evangelistic campaigns. Everybody realizes that the growth of a strong church calls for a devoted pastor and other workers who give themselves to daily ministries; but special seasons of evangelism and special efforts in the cultivation of church organizations can bring incalculable blessing.

The day has come when, upon the request of Baptist conventions and mission organizations, it is possible for the home base to assist in nation-wide evangelistic crusades, special conferences on evangelism, clinics for the strengthening of Sunday school work, special projects for the work of young people, women, and laymen, and for stewardship.

In view of the remarkable growth of Southern Baptists in our own nation and the increasing resources which God is putting into our hands for his service, we must conclude that he is calling Southern Baptists to a world task on a scale that we have not previously contemplated. When we consider the limitless possibilities that can result from sending a much greater number of missionaries, and from entering many new fields, our imaginations are kindled.

As we think of reinforcing these missionaries and national conventions with special efforts in evangelism and church development from the home base, we are filled with hope.

The future is the golden day of Baptist life. If we can wisely lay hold upon a world task, and give to it the reinforcement that should come from every New Testament church, we shall see an era of progress on a world scale.

Following the example set by our Lord, Southern Baptist missionaries have gone into the world preaching, teaching, and healing, in an effort to evangelize all who received these ministries.

The remaining chapters of this book will describe many of the approaches and means which have been used in the task of world evangelism. It will be observed that whatever means may be employed, the objectives and message remain the same.

2

Evangelism Through Preaching

IN a typical comic cartoon, a missionary usually appears wearing a rather formal black suit and perhaps a tropical sun hat as he preaches to half-clothed, primitive people in some palm-fringed village. That picture has etched itself to some degree on the minds of us all, but it is doubtful that it ever portrayed missions accurately. It is simply a comic exaggeration. Certainly, in the middle of this twentieth century it has little resemblance to reality.

The clothes that a missionary usually wears today have nothing odd or distinctive about them. The tropical sun hat is seldom seen any more. The setting in which he works is just as likely to be a town or even a large city as it is to be a small village. His hearers rarely are half-clothed savages; they are likely to be people from an ordinary cross section of life. The only element in the comic cartoon that has much realism now is the fact that the missionary is preaching. Christian missions do indeed involve preaching.

DEFINITION AND RELATIONSHIPS

In overseas mission fields, evangelism through preaching is one part of a larger undertaking. Actually, the central aim in missions is not just evangelism; rather, it is the establishment and development of strong churches. This is in no sense to minimize evangelism. After all, evangelism is basic; apart from evangelism, the establishment and development of churches would be impossible. But it is in churches that the purpose of evangelism comes to fulfilment, and it is through strong churches that continuing evangelism is projected.

Churches established on mission fields will themselves continue the work of evangelism with wider extension and greater success than would ever be possible through missionaries alone. As a matter of fact, the real hope for full evangelization of any nation in Europe, Africa, Asia, or Latin America is through churches, the fruit of missions.

This aim of planting churches requires what has been called the "larger evangelism." There is a narrow sense in which evangelism may be thought of as mere seed sowing, possibly even without much concern for results. The word is not used here in any such limited sense. Evangelism certainly means much more than widespread and perhaps random seed sowing. It is not restricted to the revival technique. The "larger evangelism" makes use of many and varied methods, not only to reach people with the gospel message, but also to secure commitment of heart and life to Christ. Evangelism in this larger sense is not considered effective until the converts are brought through baptism into fellowship and service in a New Testament church.

Preaching, in a strict sense, means formal proclaiming of the gospel of salvation; but in ordinary usage we do not limit it to that narrow sense. New Testament scholars point out a difference between *kerygma,* the proclaiming of the good news, and *didache,* the teaching of Christian doctrine and ethics to those who are saved. Most preaching combines the two.

Obviously, in these matters it is impossible to make rigid distinctions. The various chapters of this book necessarily overlap; preaching cannot and should not be divorced from teaching and healing. Preaching combines gospel proclamation and Christian instruction. Evangelism as proclamation or seed sowing merges imperceptibly into evangelism as cultivation and harvesting. Preaching and evangelism form the basis for development of churches, and those churches form bases for further preaching and evangelism. No hard and fast lines can be drawn. This chapter treats the larger evangelism through preaching in the broadest sense, and linked with the specific work of church development.

THE MISSIONARY IN GENERAL EVANGELISTIC WORK

Most evangelism in lands overseas is in the hands of nationals (both pastors and lay Christians), but the methods are substantially the same as those used by missionaries. Though the mission program centers in national Christians and their churches, this chapter describes the work largely in terms of what the missionary does, as this is representative of what his national co-workers do also.

Preaching is characteristically the function of missionaries assigned specifically to general evangelistic work, though missionaries with other assignments certainly preach, too. The missionary whose assignment is general evangelism usually divides his time between direct evangelism and church development. In discussing evangelism through preaching, we include here also the whole area of church development through the religious education program and organizational life of the churches.

In our mission literature this twofold responsibility is described by various terms: general evangelism, direct evangelism, field evangelism, or evangelism and church development. These are simply different ways of referring to the same work. The terms are used to distinguish missionaries who work primarily with churches, from those who function in relation to educational, publication, or medical institutions, or in other special services.

The task of the "field missionary" varies considerably from country to country. It depends largely upon the stage which our program has reached in any particular country. At the beginning in a new land the missionary devotes his efforts largely to pioneer evangelism. When a church is organized in his station, he likely serves as its pastor. Later the church may have a national pastor, and the missionary may direct a program of evangelism in surrounding communities. In a field where Baptist work is still more advanced, he may become an adviser to many churches, a role similar to that of the associational missionary in the United States. This development is natural and desirable. It reflects the growing strength of national leadership.

For convenience this chapter first deals specifically with preaching, and then with church development.

FORMAL PREACHING

Preaching may take forms that are not in exact accord with traditional patterns. The work done by the missionary preacher is often much like the work of the gospel preacher here in the homeland. Yet, there are differences, and the preaching ministry on the mission field has expanded in recent years in many ways.

Much preaching in overseas mission areas is formal. The trained minister, either missionary or national, delivers a prepared sermon as part of a regular preaching or worship service. The hearers may be seated on a floor of wood or even dirt and are probably dressed quite differently from American churchgoers. The words used are probably in some language other than English. A much larger proportion of the hearers will be unbelievers than is generally the case in America. The sermon is more apt to emphasize the way of salvation in clear and simple fashion. But the messenger and the message are essentially the same as in the formal preaching situations with which we are most familiar.

According to the latest report of the Foreign Mission Board, about 125 of our overseas missionaries are serving as pastors of churches. Sunday by Sunday, those pastors stand in the pulpit to proclaim the gospel. Many other missionaries who do not serve as pastors also preach in various churches frequently, or even regularly, as a part of the Sunday services.

Much more preaching is done at chapels and mission points than in churches on the mission fields. Reports show that there are more than twice as many chapels as organized churches. Many of the congregations have attractive chapel buildings; others meet in rented store-front rooms, thatch-roofed arbors, or private homes.

Many of the greatest thrills in evangelism come in the very early stages of such chapel work. Mrs. A. P. Pierson, a missionary to Mexico, recalls such an experience:

"One Sunday evening not long ago A.P. and I drove out to a little village for a service in the home of a believer. Nearly one hundred people filled the room to capacity, most of them standing during all of the meeting. After A.P. explained the plan of salvation in clear, simple words, seven adults made public professions of faith—it was the first time they had heard the gospel.

"The service ended rather late. As we finally turned toward the door, a group approached us: 'It is not too late and we have been waiting so long. Won't you please start all over again? Teach us another song of praise; then read from that Book and explain more to us—please tell us more about Jesus tonight!' "[1]

[1] "Epistles from Today's Apostles All over the World," *The Commission*, May, 1957, p. 27.

Ted Badger, missionary to the Philippines, tells of a service in a tiny bamboo house, where Missionary Bill Tisdale preached a simple gospel message, and an old woman let Jesus come into her heart:

"The light from the small kerosene lamp was dim, but all of us saw the little old woman pause just a moment. Then, straightening her bent shoulders, she resolutely stepped forward and took Bill's hand. We knew the Holy Spirit was present in that fragile bamboo house, and a flood of joy seemed to sweep over us. Even the unbelievers were strangely moved. We asked the woman her age, and she answered, 'Ninety years.'

"It is refreshing to us here in the hinterland that we do not need mighty cathedrals, stained glass windows, swelling organs, majestic choirs, polished sermons, and carpeted floors to enjoy the presence of the Almighty. Perhaps too often we trust these trappings to lead men to God, when all we need is the Word and the Spirit." [2]

Some missionaries preach in even more typically pioneer situations—in town squares, on street corners, at market places, or wherever hearers can be gathered. On mission fields there is seldom any thought of taking a religious census to locate prospects for evangelism. In most mission lands 19 out of 20 or even 99 out of 100 people are prospects for evangelism, and there are numberless millions who have never once heard the gospel. Soon after finish-

[2] "Epistles from Today's Apostles All over the World," *The Commission,* June, 1958, pp. 23, 24.

ing language study, as he began to see his many preaching opportunities, one missionary in Korea said, "I just wish there were fifty of me."

Revival meetings are a common part of the program of churches and chapels around the world. From Maiduguri, a Moslem city in Nigeria, Missionary Robert Parham reports such a service:

"Another group in Maiduguri is looking forward to a meeting tonight. The Baptist church is beginning its revival. Many have been praying that Moslems now sacrificing rams and cocks will come to know Christ. The crowd is gathering, the building is filled; but all present are Yorubas, itinerant traders from the Western Region. No Hausa Moslems are present.

"After the congregation joins in singing praises to God, an old Yoruba man, his face scarred with tribal markings, leads in prayer. The African evangelist then preaches the wonderful message of salvation. As his words reach out across the congregation and through the windows, Moslems stop out of curiosity to listen. During the invitation several Yorubas make professions of faith. The service closes with prayer in a language these Moslems understand. Only eternity will reveal the effectiveness of this service. . . ."[3]

Thus the gospel is proclaimed around the world—from church pulpit or chapel platform, in a home or on a street corner, in regular Sunday services and

[3] "Epistles from Today's Apostles All over the World," *The Commission*, June, 1958, p. 24.

in revival meetings—as missionaries and national preachers obey the command to "preach the word . . . in season, out of season" (2 Tim. 4:2).

INFORMAL PREACHING

In addition to these formal opportunities for preaching, there are times when the gospel may be proclaimed informally. Christian worship often has a profound and moving effect. Many a heart has been touched by music as the gospel is presented in congregational or special singing. Every baptism is a visual portrayal of the atoning work of Christ and the meaning of the new birth. To persons who have never seen scriptural baptism, its message can come with compelling force. The observance of the Lord's Supper points to Christ and his cross. When we recount the various means of evangelism, we include worship and the ordinances as definitely belonging in the list.

From New Testament days until now, one of the most effective means of evangelism has been personal witnessing. Great preaching does not require a large congregation. In his famous meeting with the Ethiopian, Philip is said to have "preached unto him Jesus" (Acts 8:35).

An experience told by Missionary Milton Cunningham of Southern Rhodesia is typical of the personal witness of missionaries and nationals around the world:

"Passing a group of African houses, I noticed a witch doctor's sign. Pastor Bernard (an African) and I decided to visit him. After a few introductory remarks I asked the witch doctor if he had ever heard of Jesus Christ. 'No,' he said, 'I haven't.'

"We tried to tell him who Jesus is and why he came; and then, turning to God's Word, we read several verses. After we had reviewed these things again and again, the witch doctor said:

" 'I've always known there was a God. I just didn't know he loved me.' Having given up his tools of witchcraft, he now devotes his time to spreading the good news and telling those around him that he is a Christian." [4]

This witness in words is backed up by witness in life and deeds. Every missionary shares Christ in these ways. Not all are preachers in the formal sense. Some are homemakers, and some are doctors or nurses, or lay Christians trained in other service. But all missionaries show forth the Lord Jesus in their daily lives, and all are personal soul-winners.

Many opportunities to witness come in normal everyday contacts: language students witness to their teachers; homemakers lead their servants to the Lord, or speak of Christ to vendors in the market and peddlers who come to the door; mission treasurers or business managers touch the lives of persons in business and in government. The missionary with spiritual vision finds his daily routine filled with opportunities for "evangelism through preaching" in this informal sense.

Not content with only random occasions for Christian witness, missionaries take pains to cultivate

[4] "Epistles from Today's Apostles All over the World," *The Commission*, November, 1958, p. 22.

contacts with unsaved persons. They teach English classes and Bible classes, oftentimes in their homes. They invite individuals and groups in for fellowship and for meals. Sometimes they open their homes for regular services of worship and preaching. Some special personal talent or a hobby can prove a point of contact, or the contact may be nothing more than simple friendliness and neighborliness.

A person with preconceived ideas about missions might watch a missionary day after day as he goes through the ordinary routine of life, sometimes doing very little formal preaching, and might wonder if any "mission work" is being done. Or someone with exaggerated emphasis on size and numbers might look with scornful amusement on the small gathering at some wayside preaching point. We do well to remember that any such scoffing would also have applied to Jesus, walking through the grain fields or along the seashore and giving an informal message to only twelve hearers. One is preaching, whether it be to one, or to twelve, or to a congregation that numbers a thousand.

It should be obvious, even without stating it, that most of what has been said applies to women missionaries as well as to men. The women do not engage in formal preaching, but they take part in nearly all types of informal witness that men do. This is true of missionary homemakers. It is even more true of unmarried women missionaries, who come in touch with servants and tradespeople as missionary wives do, but who have more free time for Bible classes, church responsibilities, and personal work. Men or women, preachers or laymen, married or unmarried, all find almost limitless opportunities to witness for our Lord in mission lands.

REINFORCED IMPACT

Neither the formal nor informal ways of proclaiming the gospel are new. Many are as old as the gospel itself. Nearly all have been used from the beginning of the modern missionary movement about two centuries ago. They have been thoroughly tried and proved effective. Our own day, however, has seen the development of tools and techniques that enable present-day missionaries to present the gospel with reinforced impact. Missionaries still use essentially the same proven methods, but the extent and effectiveness of those methods can be increased markedly.

The presentation of the gospel message still finds its focus in the messenger himself. There is no way to dispense with him. No matter how many tools and techniques may be multiplied, the transmission of the gospel remains fundamentally a personal matter. Delay in the spread of the gospel is not due to some technical problem or some inadequacy of method, but simply to the lack of enough messengers to reach all who need to hear.

1. *Modern transportation.* Missionaries from the beginning have practiced itineration—that is, traveling from place to place, often keeping to a regular schedule. Its possibilities have been stepped up considerably in our day. Whereas such travel on many mission fields used to be by foot or perhaps by bul-

lock cart, it is now generally by rapid modern transportation.

Motor launches are used along the rivers of Nigeria or Equatorial Brazil or Thailand. Jeeps (and their British equivalent, the Landrover) cover rugged terrain in many lands. Trains link the major cities in Europe, Japan, and other lands. Missionaries who live in cities generally have automobiles available for their use, to multiply the number of places where they can witness. Many new methods of transportation have become so common as to be taken for granted in our mission program.

More and more, as we cross the threshold of the jet age, the airplane is significant in rapid extension of the gospel. A few of our missionaries fly small mission-owned airplanes, but in most parts of the world, either adequate public transportation facilities or passable highway networks or both make the use of private planes unnecessary. Our mission-owned planes are used only in the wide expanses of Brazil, and are a possibility in parts of Africa.

Much greater use is made of regularly scheduled commercial flights. In several lands where distances are great, where plane service is dependable, and where other types of transportation are relatively poor, missionaries frequently travel by plane. Not only so, but the development of modern air travel has brought much closer contact between the Foreign Mission Board and missionaries around the world. It has also enabled pastors and other Christian leaders from America to visit mission areas and participate in special mission projects. These changes produce an approach to world missions that was out of the question thirty years ago.

2. *Audio-visual aids.* Not only do modern ways of travel enable a preacher to visit more places, but once he arrives he uses many modern techniques and machines to help him gain a hearing. In earlier days the mere presence of a missionary often was enough to attract a crowd. Foreigners were seldom seen, and people were curious about them. In most of the world today, that is no longer true. In earlier days, life was fairly simple and anything out of the ordinary would attract interest. Modern life bombards people with unusual sights and sounds until even in remote communities there are many competitors for people's attention.

The modern evangelist may use all kinds of audio-visual aids, and in some cases may use them primarily to attract hearers. For instance, W. W. Enete in Brazil and Bill Emanuel in Japan have used ventriloquism and magic. Many missionaries around the world use moving pictures to attract people. Sometimes the films deal with health and sanitation, and not necessarily with religious subjects.

Audio-visual aids are also used to present the message. Once a crowd has gathered, slides, filmstrips, or motion pictures are shown. Posters and chalk talks and object lessons may be used, too. A public address system is almost a standard part of missionary equipment. Along with it there will often be a phonograph or a tape recorder. If the audio-visual aids are to be used in rural areas or in outdoor services, there may also be a generator. Such equipment has become so commonly accepted in mission work that frequent reference is made to it with hardly a passing thought. For instance, Gene Phillips wrote from Southern Rhodesia:

"While the African Christians were going to the homes to tell the people that we had come, I was preparing for the showing of a filmstrip. My projector had been wired so that I could use the electricity from my car battery. I also had a tape recorder and a converter.

"By the time I was ready, many people had gathered to see the Bible story of Noah and the ark. Some had traveled for many miles and afterwards spent the night in Gutu.

"The service began with hymns; prayer, Scripture reading, comments, and a few announcements followed. Then the filmstrip, with the narration in the language of the people, was shown. I had prepared the narration tape with the help of an African teacher and had included music and sound effects.

"After the film an invitation was given. With only a flashlight in my hand for light I saw twenty-two people indicate a profession of faith in Jesus as Lord and Saviour. Joy flooded my soul and thanks were given to God for his mighty love and work." [5]

Missionary Tom Clinkscales wrote from Brazil:

"A short time ago in Maringa I held services at night, using films and filmstrips from the Atlas News Service, the South Brazil Baptist Mission's news and information agency. During the day we held a Bible

[5] Gene D. Phillips, "Epistles from Today's Apostles All over the World," *The Commission*, March, 1958, p. 22.

crusade in the city. At the beginning we visited the mayor, presented him with a Bible, and secured permission to use the public-address system and to sell Bibles." [6]

In Japan, missionaries and their national co-workers have conducted campaigns advertised as "music evangelism," publicizing the use of a Hammond organ, a vibraharp, and other instruments.

3. *Mass communications media.* In principle, there is nothing new about "mass communications." Ever since the invention of printing, such communication has been possible through the printed word. From the beginning of modern missions the publication of Bibles and tracts has been a standard mission operation, and the gospel in that printed form has reached places and people who have never seen or heard a preacher in person.

Still today the work of the Bible societies is indispensable. Though there are some lands where Baptist missions publish their own Bibles, in most mission areas we depend entirely upon the work of Bible societies. Through reading rooms, through booths at fairs and expositions, through colportage work, and through many other channels, Bibles and tracts move out to reinforce the impact of the gospel. Tremendous numbers of tracts have been distributed in connection with evangelistic campaigns. A typical example is reported by Missionary Hiram Duffer in Mexico:

"Thirty teams of two people each visited in the

[6] Gene H. Wise, "Evangelical Christianity Versus Traditional Religion," *The Commission,* July, 1957, p. 11.

homes of the area, each team going into from five to ten homes each afternoon. The visitors distributed 25,000 tracts and 450 New Testaments. The Testaments were left with the understanding that they could be kept if the recipient showed interest in the gospel when a pastor or other visitor returned. If no interest was evident the Testament would be given to someone else. Little cardboard door-and-window signs reading, '*En Cristo Hay Paz*' ('In Christ There Is Peace'), were also distributed."[7]

Newspapers are another traditional means of mass communication, and newspaper advertising has been prominent in the evangelistic approach in some lands. The testimony of a young convert in Indonesia could be matched by many similar experiences. He explains in his own words:

"One day I happened to pick up a daily newspaper; and it said, 'Pastor Pormes, of Calvary Baptist Church, cordially invites people to Bible classes and preaching services on Sunday.' I read and reread it. There was something about it that told me I must go and hear this. The Spirit of the Lord seemed to compel me to go.

"The next Sunday found me seated with many other people in Calvary Baptist Church. This was the first time I had been to any service in many years. There that day I felt Jesus knocking on the door of my heart and by his great help I opened the door and let him come in."[8]

[7] "Foreign Mission News: Mexico," *The Commission*, January, 1957, p. 25.
[8] "We Saw God Do It," *The Commission*, April, 1958, p. 27.

Now these earlier mass communication methods which made possible the spread of the printed word are being supplemented by new inventions for the broadcasting of the spoken and even the visual message.

The use of radio in evangelism is commonplace in almost every land. Sometimes the broadcasts are local, sometimes over stations with national or even international coverage. Two annual reports will indicate something of the scope and possibilities of radio evangelism in overseas missions. One is from Edward Berry, who is responsible for Baptist radio and recording work in Brazil:

"A total of 303 programs were prepared and transmitted over three radio stations. At present all of these are recorded in our studios. Thirty-one dramatized Bible stories were recorded. Christmas skits and poems were also prepared by our cast. Eight new gospel records were produced and placed on the market; over twenty thousand records were sold during the year." [9]

The other report comes from Frank and Margaret Mitchell who work in Chile:

"The radio is an increasingly effective means of evangelism. The Chilean 'Baptist Hour,' heard through the year on seven stations from Arice in the extreme north to Osorno in the south, reaches an estimated twenty-five thousand each Sunday. 'Bible Correspondence Courses,' conducted by R. Cecil Moore in connection with the radio program, have enrolled seventeen hundred students. Several con-

[9] *The Field Is the World,* 1957, p. 42.

versions, two calls to the ministry, and some reclamations have been reported as a result of this ministry."[10]

Thus far, television has been used only slightly in Southern Baptist missions overseas. But as television becomes more common in other lands, it can be used to carry the gospel to the homes and the hearts of many, many thousands who otherwise would not hear.

4. *Special group approaches.* The evangelistic impact has been reinforced also by some special approaches to certain selected groups. In some lands, for instance, rural areas offer unusual hindrances to evangelism and require a special approach. The Foreign Mission Board has appointed a few agriculture experts whose ministry helps open a door for evangelism in rural areas.

In every mission land, missionaries and national Christians give special attention to people who are unable to attend ordinary church services. Evangelistic preaching in prisons, orphanages, and old people's homes, evangelistic visitation in hospitals, and other similar ministries are typical.

Vacation Bible schools are a fruitful evangelistic agency. In fields like Mexico and the Philippines, the schools often act as the first opening wedge for Christian work in communities that otherwise would be antagonistic.

Another special approach that is becoming increasingly prominent is work with college and university students, who usually are more open-minded

[10] *Ibid.*, p. 45.

and more interested in the gospel than the general population. Furthermore, the student group is strategic because it comprises the future leaders of entire nations. In lands where there are no Baptist colleges, the best-trained leadership for Baptist church and denominational life will come from among the students in private and government universities.

The Foreign Mission Board promotes student centers near great universities, where they may minister to literally tens of thousands of students. The purpose is largely evangelistic; but where there are Baptist students the center serves also as a focus for a program similar to our Baptist Student Union in America. Activities attractive to students—music, recreation, discussion groups, English classes, Bible classes, devotional meetings, and the like—all may be used as means of initial contact with students who can then be reached with the gospel.

More and more, the Foreign Mission Board is appointing trained and experienced workers for this type of service. In a few places, because of unusual conditions, there are even Baptist student dormitories near the universities, to provide living arrangements under Christian auspices for students coming from other cities. A prominent example is a Baptist student dormitory at Chihuahua, Mexico.

5. *Mass evangelism.* One of the most remarkable reinforcements of the evangelistic impact recently has been in the area of mass evangelism. A plan used with marked success is the entry into some new city in force. Instead of a small and slow begin-

ning with a little mission on a side street and only one or two workers, new work is begun in such a way as to bring it to the attention of the entire city. Thrilling results came from such an approach in Asahikawa, Japan. The method has been used also in other places. An example from Brazil indicates what is involved:

"Baptists had no work in Cachoeira do Sul, a city of thirty thousand people in the state of Rio Grande do Sul, Brazil, until early this year when nine theological students, five pastors, and about twenty volunteer workers went there for eight days of intensive evangelistic effort. Now Baptist work is firmly established in the city, though there is no full-time director available.

"During the campaign five street meetings were held in different sections of town each day; and main meetings were held in the public square, in the very heart of town, each evening. Baptists had a radio program and an average of twenty spot announcements each day on each of the two local stations. The city was sown with posters, handbills, and tracts. Three, and sometimes four, automobiles roamed the town for hours each day announcing the meetings.

"Two-hour instruction and inspirational meetings were held daily for the workers. Preaching in the various meetings was done by the seminary students.

"The revival meetings resulted in more than a thousand decisions of one kind or another. All of these came to the front; but with many it was manifestations of interest rather than definite decisions. About two hundred gave their names and addresses; and these were visited by campaign workers during the week." [11]

Simultaneous evangelistic campaigns in many churches in the same city, or even in a much broader area, are promoted frequently. For several years the Foreign Mission Board has stimulated campaigns of this sort by making available special funds for advance projects in evangelism and church development. Such projects have enabled Southern Baptists with outstanding experience in evangelism to contribute greatly to evangelistic efforts overseas.

Specialists have helped in the planning stages of evangelistic campaigns in Japan and Argentina. Sometimes the team for a simultaneous crusade has included two or three preachers from the United States and several missionaries and national pastors from nearby nations. This was the case in outstanding campaigns both in Hong Kong and in Taiwan (Formosa).

Mass evangelistic crusades conducted as advance projects on mission fields have used all the techniques with which we are most familiar. Experience shows that the principles which apply in such campaigns in the United States apply also in other parts of the world. Human nature is essentially the same everywhere.

To be sure, there are local conditions which call for adjustments in plans and approaches. Churches

[11] "Foreign Mission News: Brazil," *The Commission,* October, 1957, p. 14.

and conventions made up of Asians or Africans or Latin Americans have their own customs, methods, and points of view. They do not adopt schemes that are "made in America" without changes to suit their own temperaments, needs, and circumstances. Baptists around the world, though, are eager to learn new ways of evangelism; and Southern Baptists are joining with them in advance projects which reinforce the impact of the gospel.

CHURCH DEVELOPMENT

As stated earlier, evangelism and church development go hand in hand. When preaching bears its expected fruit, there are converts to be organized into churches and trained in Christian service. The work of church development was not always as well appreciated, either on the mission fields or in the homeland, as it is today.

The role of the preacher was once thought of almost entirely in terms of formal preaching. He has a whole added area of responsibility today for leading in the development of a strong church. This involves religious education, stewardship, organization, promotion, and church fellowship. More of a pastor's time is often taken with church development functions than with sermon preparation and preaching.

The time of a missionary who is assigned to general evangelism is divided between the presentation of the gospel and the development of churches. In his responsibility for church growth, he has a many-sided role, just as does a pastor in the United States.

The missionary leads in stimulating and guiding the gospel outreach of the young churches through programs of visitation, the opening of new mission points, and other evangelistic projects.

Teaching plays a large part in the responsibility of the overseas missionary. Most members of his congregation will have almost no background knowledge of the Bible and Christian truth. A vital part of his ministry lies in the doctrinal study classes for inquirers and new believers that are a usual part of preparation for baptism and church membership in mission areas.

Again the missionary plays an important part in developing the organizational life of the churches, applying the principles of religious education to simple pioneer situations in terms of the experience and the culture of the people. Similar guidance of church finance also is essential.

Much of this work is done through private conference or committee meetings, and the major part of a missionary's time may be taken up, and quite profitably, by such meetings.

Missionary women who are assigned to general evangelism naturally do not have pastoral functions. Their work in relation to church development resembles that of educational and youth workers in churches of the homeland.

Church growth on the mission field, even more than in the United States, depends on pastoral leadership and example, because the churches generally have few lay members with long experience in church activities.

1. *A church development pattern.* There is much similarity in the process of church development anywhere. It starts with a decision to open a mission point in some new community. Usually there is a sponsoring church, but sometimes the new work is a home mission project of an association or convention. A missionary may have major responsibility, or he may be simply counselor to a national preacher who is responsible for the work.

Before a new church can be developed, there are many practical problems to solve. These include a place of meeting, living arrangements for the worker, elements of the program to be projected, financing, relationships of the work to the sponsoring church, and the most suitable time and manner for beginning.

Perhaps a small nucleus of Christians has lived in the community from the first. Often, however, the work starts "from scratch" with Bible teaching and gospel preaching. After a time, converts are won, and these are instructed and prepared for baptism. Eventually, the converts organize a new Baptist church.

Probably by this time serious study has been given to the question of a permanent location for the young church. The people do what they can to secure land and a building, often with help from the Baptist association or convention in the area and from the Foreign Mission Board.

Gradually the church grows stronger until it needs no outside help or guidance. Long before it reaches that point, it usually shows its own missionary concern by opening mission points in still other communities.

If a missionary has major responsibility for this development, he perhaps will have a furlough due by the time the church is well established. Some other leader, most likely a national pastor, replaces him; then after furlough he may start the same process in a new location. Or he may work with two or more chapels continually, helping them develop normally into strong churches.

2. *Advance projects.* Within recent decades Southern Baptists have learned to appreciate the tremendous value of a progressive religious education program. Church organizations for evangelism, enlistment, Bible study, training in church membership, and missionary education have proved a major factor in the rapid growth of Southern Baptists. Similar educational and promotional principles are now being applied to the areas of church administration and stewardship and finance.

All of these means of church and denominational growth are a growing part of the life of young churches and Baptist denominations in mission areas around the world. Missionaries find many of their finest opportunities in this realm, as they help churches to have strong organizations for effective religious education. In this way the churches are enabled, not only to conserve the fruits of evangelism, but also to direct their full resources toward sharing the gospel with still others.

As indicated already, the Foreign Mission Board promotes special "advance projects" in evangelism and church development. The projects not only reinforce the impact of gospel preaching through city-wide crusades and simultaneous evangelistic campaigns, but also strengthen religious education and help develop strong churches more quickly.

As a part of these projects, highly respected experts on various church organizations have visited mission fields to share the lessons that we in the homeland have learned about church development. These trips have been made by specialists in Sunday school, Training Union, Woman's Missionary Union and Brotherhood work, stewardship and church finance, student work, radio and television, church architecture—all for projects in church development.

As with the evangelism projects, experience shows that the same church development principles used in the United States are effective also in other lands around the world. Details of their application vary. Methods are adapted to national cultures and local situations. Initiative in planning rests with the churches and the associations or conventions. Certainly, there is no attempt to compel national Baptist groups to adopt American methods. But Baptists everywhere are showing a desire to know more about methods that have proved effective.

The progress made possible by advance projects and by a general upsurge of interest in the organizational and promotional life of the churches, should be considered a major forward step in our overseas mission program since World War II.

ENLISTING AND LEADING OTHERS

In this entire matter of evangelism through preaching and church development, what the missionary himself does is not nearly as important as his example and his leadership among national Christians.

In new mission fields, young converts gain their first ideas about Christian witness from missionaries. People in many parts of the world are accustomed to learning through observation and imitation. New Christians learn to do the things they see the missionaries doing. Often, the missionary leads in house-to-house visitation, tract distribution, and other ways of personal witness.

Even in mission lands of greater maturity, where there are many strong churches and national leaders, the influence of missionaries is still extremely important. Their concern and activities help to define the role of the Christian leader in the thinking of young national preachers. The missionary who makes full use of this stewardship of personal example and leadership will accomplish far more than he ever could simply through his own personal preaching and work of church development.

This is especially true in dealing with students in the seminary, where they learn to take an active part in personal soul-winning and evangelistic outreach. An example is seen in the following report from the International Baptist Theological Seminary in Colombia:

"When the seminary's dramatics class presented

a missionary play, Señor Padilla constructed all the necessary scenery and played one of the most important roles. At the conclusion of this presentation an invitation was given and twenty-three young people came forward making decisions for Christ, some surrendering for special service.

"Other students put their seminary studies into practice by teaching in local churches or working in missions or preaching points on week ends. One of these began evangelistic work in Pereira with three persons. Seven months later he reported a Sunday school attendance of sixty. There were twenty-seven persons in a class of new believers . . ." [12]

Another typical incident is described by Missionary Carl Hunker, a teacher in the Taiwan Baptist Theological Seminary:

"Today was Missionary Day. This morning we felt new courage as faculty and students gathered together for inspiration and prayer with regard to the Lord's commission. This afternoon and evening we felt strong in the faith as teachers and students divided into groups and went out into the streets for street preaching. Many heard, many more accepted gospel tracts, a few manifested genuine interest in the Word. Like the seventy in their return to the Master, we returned to the school tonight enthusiastic and zealous for his work." [13]

On Sundays and during vacations, seminary students fan out individually and in groups over large areas to preach and witness. Often they reach into

[12] "Serving While Studying," *The Commission*, July, 1958, p. 5.
[13] Carl Hunker, letter, October 22, 1958.

communities that are not touched by the ordinary work of missionaries or churches. Sometimes they cross national boundaries, as, for instance, in the case of students in the international Baptist seminary at Zurich, Switzerland, who preach in southern Germany.

There is continuous training and encouragement in evangelism, both for lay Christians and for ministers. Churches offer classes in personal soul-winning. Handbooks for soul-winners are placed in the hands of church members. Leaders gather for spiritual retreats and evangelistic conferences. A conference reported from Southern Rhodesia is representative:

"Nineteen of the sixty-four African pastors and laymen who attended the evangelistic conference in Southern Rhodesia this year made public decisions, some rededicating their lives and others saying they felt definitely that God was calling them into the gospel ministry.

"The four-day conference was held at the African Baptist Theological Seminary, near Gwelo, Southern Rhodesia. During the mornings there were seminars on 'Deepening the Spiritual Life' and 'How to Win Men to Christ' and an inspirational message. Afternoons were devoted to conferences and organized recreation, and the evening programs included group singing and another inspirational message." [14]

All this process of enlisting and leading others means that as time passes national Christians take

[14] "Foreign Mission News: Southern Rhodesia," *The Commission*, October, 1957, p. 21.

an ever larger place in the total picture of evangelism through preaching. Even on pioneer mission fields and in young churches, it is not long before most converts come through the witness of new Christians. Their zeal is often such as to put us to shame. Missionary Lolete Dotson, of Nigeria, has told of a new convert going back to his home village and returning two weeks later with a list of twenty-five people to whom he had spoken about Christ. Thousands of stories could be told of new believers inviting members of their family and friends and witnessing to them earnestly until they also believe.

Most churches overseas are eager to sponsor mission points in other communities. Lay members of young churches that may have less than fifty members travel many miles each Sunday afternoon to direct Sunday schools, conduct services, and preach the gospel in mission chapels.

Lay preaching and lay responsibility in evangelism are far more common on the mission field than in America. American church life is sometimes compared rather unfavorably with that of New Testament times, in that we now tend to employ a preacher to do our Christian witnessing. In this regard churches in mission areas are much nearer the New Testament spirit and practice. Lay Christians on mission fields assume that it is normal for a Christian to testify and preach.

This same quality permeates the life of young Baptist associations and conventions. Even though they may lack in numbers or financial resources, and may not have highly trained leadership, associations and conventions on the mission field generally have a vigorous missionary spirit. They assume heavy responsibilities in the evangelization of their own homelands, sometimes through a formal Home Mission Board, as in Brazil. They share in sending the gospel beyond their own borders, not only through prayers and gifts, but sometimes by formal mission programs. For many years Brazilian Baptists have worked in Portugal. More recently the Baptists of Japan have undertaken a similar mission project in Okinawa.

Because this book is intended for Southern Baptist readers, it centers attention on the missionary representatives whom we send out. But for a better balanced understanding, we need to think of national Christians as doing most of the work of evangelism, and assuming increasing initiative, responsibility, and leadership in it, with encouragement and help from our missionaries.

One essential and universal element in the process of evangelism through preaching has been only barely mentioned in this chapter. That element is prayer. Reports from the fields are full of phrases like this: "after weeks of witness and prayer"; "prayer for a spirit-inspired revival"; "the Lord is answering prayer"; "a couple for whom we have been praying very earnestly." Always and everywhere prayer and witness, prayer and preaching, go together. Whatever means may be used for proclaiming the gospel (and we use more and more different methods), the power and the results come from God in answer to prayer.

3

Evangelism Through Teaching

GOVERNMENTS in all parts of the world are trying to satisfy the hunger of the masses for education. Usually they have welcomed the efforts of Christian missions to provide their people with an opportunity for education, and children throng the mission schools in some countries. Almost five hundred applicants appeared not long ago at a Baptist girls' school in Agbor, Nigeria, which was able to accept only thirty new students.

According to Missionary William S. Wester (*The Commission*, September, 1956, p. 19): "Africans in Rhodesia are hungry physically, spiritually, and mentally—but most of all they seem to be hungry for education. . . . To educate is not our chief aim. Our purpose is to fulfil the Great Commission. To strike a blow for God is our desire. This end we seek: indigenous Baptist churches in Rhodesia and this section of Africa."

If this is to be accomplished, Mr. Wester continued, it must be through educated and trained leaders. For this reason, we set up schools to teach those hungry to learn, to win them through the love of Jesus, to train them, and to challenge them to serve

Christ with the knowledge and training they have acquired.

God did not intend for man to grope along in the darkness of ignorance and superstition. He gave him the ability to learn. His purpose was for man to find the ultimate truth in Jesus Christ the Son of God. All truths that the mind of man is capable of comprehending are overshadowed by that great central truth.

Most people believe that education leads to a better way of life. Usually it does, although highly educated people in underdeveloped areas occasionally find that opportunities to use their specialized training are too limited by conditions around them.

Three out of five people in the world's population can neither read nor write. Think of how much they miss that is of real worth! The world's literature is closed to them. The Bible is a closed book to them. The blessing of reading and understanding such basic documents as the Declaration of Independence, the Constitution of the United States, and the United Nations' Declaration of Human Rights is denied them. As life grows more and more complicated, it becomes increasingly difficult for those who cannot read and write to get along at all.

Missionary James L. Garrett, North Brazil, reports an interesting experience in conducting a Vacation Bible school. When time for the first session came, the workers—all of them volunteers—reported on schedule. Imagine Garrett's surprise when he learned that not a single one of the workers was able to read the materials they were to present that day.

The children were sent home and asked to report at the same time the next day. In the meantime, the volunteer workers were taught the stories by rote!

Eager young people will go to almost any length to secure an education. In lands where the standard of living is much lower than our own, large families can hardly hope to send all of the children to school. By working together, they may be able to provide for the education of one member of the family.

According to the most recent report of the Foreign Mission Board, Southern Baptists operate nine hundred (using round numbers) schools which enrol 129,800 students. The major share of schools and students are found in Nigeria. Only three hundred of the nearly fifty-three hundred teachers are missionaries. The schools include kindergartens, elementary schools, secondary schools, colleges, women's training schools, theological seminaries, and institutes.

The schools in Nigeria provide education on the kindergarten, elementary, secondary, teacher training, and theological levels. Almost all of the teachers who instruct the eighty thousand pupils in the elementary schools are Nigerians. Some missionaries are attached to the staffs of the twenty-four secondary schools which enrol approximately twenty-four hundred students. Many graduates of the elementary and secondary schools find their way to the seminary for theological training. Six teacher training centers that specialize in the preparation of teachers enrol almost seven hundred students.

NONTHEOLOGICAL EDUCATION

The fundamental purpose of nontheological education on the mission field is to lead people to a saving knowledge of Jesus Christ and to develop Christian character. This purpose is achieved through direct evangelistic and devotional activities. Christian teachers, Bible classes, and chapel programs help to keep the emphasis centered on evangelism.

Some schools also have chaplains, Baptist student organizations, weeks of religious emphases and home visitation programs. Missionary faculty members have frequent opportunity to guide young people by counseling and by personal example.

Baptist schools are necessary for various reasons. A Baptist constituency must be developed in every land. State-supported schools either may be too few or be inadequate. Baptist children are sometimes persecuted or discriminated against in other than Baptist schools. Future Baptist leaders can best be prepared in Baptist schools.

Contributions made to the Christian cause by Baptist mission schools include students, parents, and teachers won to the Lord; greater good will and respect for evangelical Christianity; a better-educated Baptist constituency; influence exerted in circles not ordinarily reached by the churches; greater stability for Baptist work; and the training of church and denominational leaders.

Mission schools are not free from problems. As a matter of fact, the problems occasionally seem to outweigh the advantages. Current operating expenses and capital needs amount to a great deal. Unless a school's administration is constantly vigilant, the secular aspects of education may be allowed to overbalance the evangelistic purpose. A poorly conducted school may be detrimental to the Baptist witness. Care must always be taken that missionary effort be applied where it will do the most good. It is often difficult to secure from among the nationals Christian teachers who share the same idealism and motivation as the missionaries. Then, there is the temptation to look to governments for financial aid—a temptation which must be resisted even when teachers and other staff members may be clamoring for pay increases which slim mission budgets cannot afford.

The ideal is for schools to be supported completely by national or local Baptists. They should not look to the Foreign Mission Board indefinitely for financial assistance. When a school which has been receiving aid assumes its own support, the Board is able to help others.

Scholarship funds of mission schools necessarily are somewhat limited, but a number of deserving students are given help each year. The students must give evidence of a willingness to work, considerable scholastic ability, and a definite interest in church life.

Mission schools vary from country to country. Their size varies from small ventures to large educational projects enrolling thousands of students. Schools enrolling more than one thousand, however, are comparatively few. Each school's curriculum is set up to meet the requirements demanded by its national government, so that schools vary in that respect. But the mission school curriculum always adds Bible study.

Visitors to some mission areas are often surprised to learn that pupils in mission schools wear uniforms. One useful purpose of uniforms is to assure that parents will provide adequate clothing for their children. Another advantage is that children who might not be able to dress well are not placed at a disadvantage by those who can.

While it is not universally the rule, many mission schools require a certain amount of manual work from each student each week. Additional work is often done to pay school fees.

Churches often sponsor and conduct elementary schools. This is true in Colombia, Nigeria, and elsewhere. In fact, a tremendous number of elementary schools in Nigeria are operated in this way. The pastor of the Baptist church in the port city of Limon, Costa Rica, a graduate of the American Baptist Theological Seminary in Nashville, Tennessee, is also director of a Baptist school for English-speaking West Indians.

Sometimes mission schools serve as models for other schools in their area. The Baptist academy, Temuco, Chile, for example, pioneered in the field of coeducation in that section of Chile. The coeducational idea is now generally accepted there.

There is ample evidence that these schools do evangelize. The Baptist school, Beirut, Lebanon, is said to contribute to the Baptist witness through the general spirit of Christian love and fellowship it radiates. Missionary Tom G. Hall, reporting from the Sanyati Reserve in Southern Rhodesia, comments about the boarding school there: "Many of the students have come to know Jesus in the past year. Not a student has left the school in the past three years without having made a profession of faith in Christ. A number of these have been won to the Lord by their schoolmates."

In Nazareth, Israel, the church works in close cooperation with primary and secondary schools. Missionary Herman L. Petty, after five years of service there, is convinced of their worth. He submits the following personal testimonies to show what the Nazareth school has meant to three young people:

First student: "The best thing I noticed during the four years I was at the Baptist school was that every morning at eight o'clock the students and teachers entered the church. We remained in the chapel for half an hour praising the Lord. Every day someone preached the gospel to us, and often an invitation was given us to accept Christ as personal Saviour. Every Sunday I also attended the church to hear God's Word preached. One Sunday I, along with two of my friends, made my decision to follow Christ."

Second student: "Before I came to this school, I didn't know anything about Jesus Christ. But when I came, I learned many things which I did not know before. It was in my third year that I had my experience with Christ. One night, after seeking the Lord,

I dreamed I heard the voice of Jesus calling me to accept him as Saviour. When I awoke I promised to give my heart to him and always to be his. That night was wonderful for me, for Jesus came into my heart."

Third student: "When I was fourteen years old I entered the Baptist school in Nazareth. There I began hearing about Christ, and soon I began feeling my need for him to help me in my lessons and in my attitude toward others. After a period of time I accepted the Lord Jesus with all my heart. I wept much for my sins. Now I feel my daily life is changed and I feel inner gladness and happiness. I have had success in many things in which I had failed before. Thank God for this school, its teachers, and its spirit."

High schools and colleges have been established in several countries. The Japan Baptist Convention has a university and girls' college with nearly six thousand students. Special attention is given there to the training of kindergarten teachers for school work. Hong Kong Baptist College was opened in 1956, with 150 students enrolled the first year. More than 250 students from 48 schools in Hong Kong and Macao took entrance examinations hoping to be admitted. An outstanding Christian layman, business man, and Baptist world leader, Dr. Lam Chi Fung, is the president of the college.

SPECIAL APPROACHES

Special educational approaches are sometimes necessary in order to cope with specific needs which apparently cannot be met otherwise. Adult illiterates, for obvious reasons, find it impossible to attend an ordinary school. Literacy campaigns are often just what is needed.

Not nearly all Baptist believers can read. Dr. Frank C. Laubach, the literacy specialist, has visited many mission areas in order to teach people to read their Bibles. One of his most recent visits was to Spain, where he gave encouragement to an ambitious program of teaching illiterate believers to read their Bibles. Those who have had the experience say there are few joys equal to that of teaching an adult to read his Bible. The gratitude of the newly literate person usually is overwhelming.

Schools such as industrial institutes combine direct evangelism and education with a program of technical training. An example is the institute in Corrente, Brazil, one of the most remote mission stations in the world. (Its remoteness is due to difficulty of access rather than distance from large urban centers.) The program of the Corrente institute includes primary school, secondary school, training in industrial arts, and a demonstration farm system which also contributes to the support of the school.

The Kate White Domestic School, in Salvador, Brazil, is unique in that it is the only one of its kind maintained by Southern Baptists anywhere in the world. The name indicates its primary emphasis on domestic arts. It seeks to build better homes through practical instruction and Christian idealism.

Good Will Centers are also educational institutions. They are more than educational institutions, to be sure, but their educational function should not be overlooked. The oldest Centers are in Latin America and in Tobata, Japan.

The Good Will Center in Rio de Janeiro, Brazil, may serve as an example of these mission Centers. It opens at seven in the morning and does not close until nine-thirty at night. Among its courses of study are literacy, cooking, child care, music, English, Bible and doctrines, and crafts. Like most Good Will Centers, it is in a densely populated, underprivileged section of the city. The Good Will Center in Antofagasta, Chile, combines these ordinary Center activities with a clinic, grade school, and fully functioning Baptist church. The pastor is himself a product of the Good Will Center's activities. The Good Will Center in Rosario, Argentina, like those elsewhere, offers a variety of classes for adults, young people, and children. A great many homes are reached directly through its ministry.

Dar es Salaam, Tanganyika, is one of Southern Baptists' newest stations of work. There, a week-day adult education and social center offers classes in Bible, literature, sewing, hygiene, and other subjects.

Schools of nursing are usually termed medical mission work because they are conducted in connection with mission hospitals. They contribute to both the medical and evangelistic work. A nursing school usually develops a short while after a hospital is in operation.

One of the most interesting types of mission work is what has come to be called "student work," and one of its particularly interesting branches is the student home work in Mexico. Evangelical schools under foreign leadership are prohibited in Mexico. Since Baptists cannot conduct schools of their own there, they provide homes for students who wish to study in state or national high schools and universities.

The student homes provide a Christian environment for young people who, for the first time, are away from home and customary religious influences. There are daily devotional periods at the home, and the students are given every encouragement to participate actively in the local church.

"The communistic and atheistic teachings in the classroom confuse many students," says Mrs. Coy Lee Pierson, one of our missionaries, "and we are ready to answer their questions with our Bibles open. In that way we train them to search the Scriptures for the truth, and they are prepared to choose the right and discard the false teachings.

"The majority of nonbelievers who come to the student homes accept Christ as their personal Saviour during the first year. A good percentage of them dedicate their lives to full-time Christian service and go from us to the Baptist theological seminary in Torreon, where they prepare for the ministry or for missionary service."

Mrs. Pierson tells how the student homes in the city of Chihuahua, Mexico, got their start:

"Jorge, a lad of fourteen, walked up to me during an associational meeting and asked, 'May I live in your home and go to school?' This boy is the old-

Rachel Colvin

Devotional service at the Baptist Student Home for Girls, Guadalajara, Mexico, with one of the girls leading

Missionary J. J. Cowsert examining finished Bibles at the Baptist Publishing House, Rio de Janeiro

Rachel Colvin

Baptist Church, Chihuahua, Mexico

Morris Wright, **Jr.**

In the Theological Department, Seinan Gakuin, Fukuoka, Japan, with Professor Toshio Miyoshi teaching Greek class

Fon H. Scofield, Jr.

Centocello Baptist Church, Rome, Italy; choir composed of young people from George B. Taylor Home

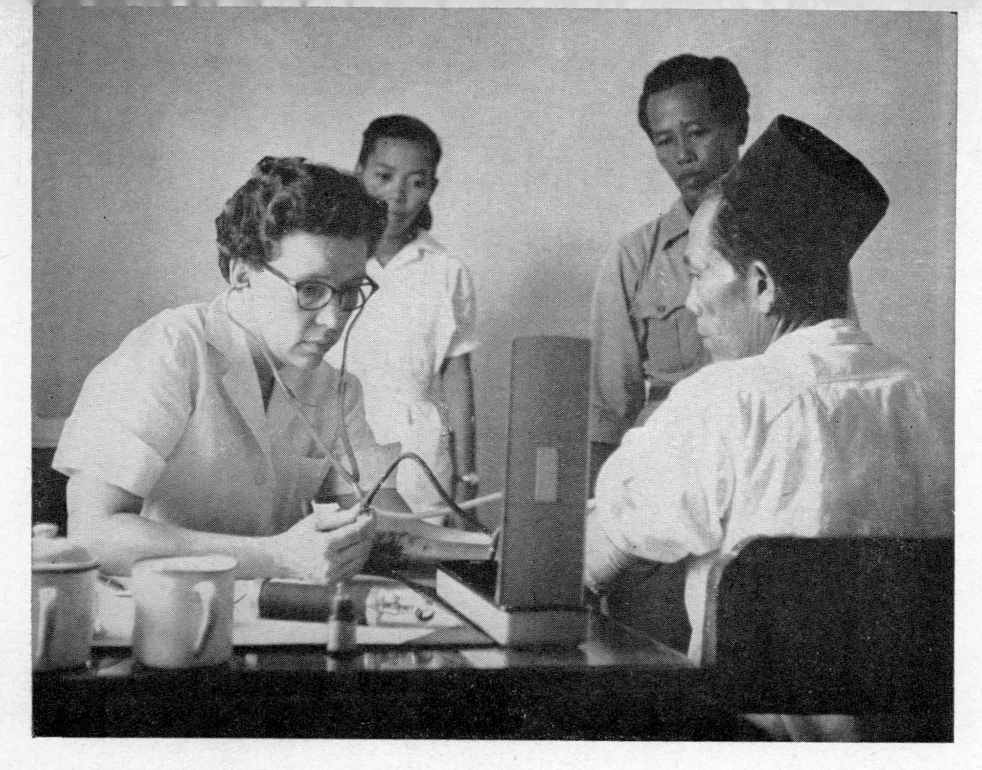

Dr. Kathleen Jones, missionary, checking Moslem patient at Baptist Hospital, Kediri, Indonesia

Missionary Marion Moorhead baptizing a young man in the river, Sapporo area, Japan

Gerald Harvey

Southern Baptist missionaries studying Swahili language at Dar es Salaam, Tanganyika; left to right: Mr. and Mrs. Webster Carroll, Mr. and Mrs. James Hampton, Mr. and Mrs. Samuel DeBord, and Mr. and Mrs. Earl Martin est son of a couple who had just surrendered to the mission call and were on their way to live among the Indians who live high in the mountains of Chihuahua State.

"If Jorge's parents were willing to go off to an isolated place to win one of the most backward tribes of Indians in all North America, then I should count it a real privilege to open my home to the son who wanted to study. He returned to Chihuahua with us and shared our son's bedroom.

"One boy's coming led other boys to believe that they, too, would be welcome in our home while pursuing a formal education that was not offered in towns other than this capital city."

The Pierson home also made room for girls who wished to pursue an education, even though it meant that the daughter had to share her room with three other girls.

The Anahuac Student Homes in Chihuahua are now thriving institutions, located on a spacious property upon which very attractive buildings have been constructed. They provide living facilities for up to sixty young men and forty-eight girls.

Other student homes in Mexico are the Boys' Home and the Mae Davis Memorial Home (for girls) in Guadalajara, the University Student Home in Mexico City, and Guerrero Student Home in Iguala.

Student centers are being established in many countries of the Orient. Taiwan (Formosa) has student work in three university centers. Five missionaries are teaching in government schools as a means of contact with students. A Baptist student center located on the campus of the University of Hawaii has the usual Baptist Student Union program, and in addition offers Bible classes and operates a hostel for students from outside Honolulu.

Despite their broad educational background, missionaries themselves are not through with school when they are appointed for foreign service. When they serve in a foreign-language area, language study is a "must," although the actual procedure varies around the world. Almost every mission now has its own language school or takes advantage of language schools already in operation.

Missionary appointees destined for Spanish-speaking areas attend language school in Costa Rica; the school, in the city of San Jose, is under the control and direction of the Presbyterian Church, U.S.A. Missionary appointees designated for service in Portuguese-speaking Brazil attend language school in Campinas, Sao Paulo, Brazil; the school is operated on a co-operative basis by two Presbyterian denominations, the Methodists, and Southern Baptists.

The Nigerian mission maintains the Newton Memorial School for missionary children and a language and orientation school for missionaries.

Missionaries to Arab-speaking countries usually study the language at the American School in Beirut, Lebanon. The mission in Indonesia set up a language school within a few years after entering the country. In the Philippines, the Southern Baptist mission itself grew out of the Chinese language school that was transferred there from Communist-dominated northern China.

LEADERSHIP TRAINING

When education is neglected by Christian missions, the fruits of their labor are stunted. "In our zeal to evangelize," writes Missionary James P. Kirk of South Brazil, "we have neglected to indoctrinate our people. As a consequence we have not produced adequate leadership, either on the lay level or on the pastoral level."

In an effort to overcome the situation, he has launched a program of training. It includes brief training clinics or institutes at the associational level; spiritual retreats for groups such as the pastors, lay preachers, the Sunday school, the Training Union, and missionary organizations; Christian life conferences; and an extension course for pastors.

The ability to read is not all that is required if one is to understand the Word of God. The Ethiopian eunuch (Acts 8:26-40) could read, but he could not understand what he was reading. He required someone to help him understand the message. It is at this point that leadership training is so important.

Regional Bible institutes for laymen are conducted in Guatemala. The basic plan involves selection of a central meeting place, a faculty made up jointly of missionaries and national pastors, and a simple and practical course of study covering one week. Each person who participates pays a small registration fee and brings four pounds of beans, corn, chicken, or some other food.

The course includes Bible study, personal soul-winning, simple preaching, and Sunday school lesson preparation. In the afternoons the students go out two-by-two to do personal work.

As Missionary Clark Scanlon says, "These short courses do not take the place of theological seminaries, but they do help the man who is in charge of a mission, the woman who needs training in teaching methods or Vacation Bible school work, the young person who wants to know how to win others to Christ, and every person who wants to be a better church member."

National departments of religious education exert a helpful influence upon churches in some countries. The pattern may change from place to place, but the purpose is the same. Usually there are departments of Sunday school, Training Union, and Woman's Missionary Union. The youth organizations of Woman's Missionary Union also receive due attention.

Another promotional approach is made through provincial or state conventions within some of the larger countries. The state of Pernambuco in Brazil is an illustration. Reports from the Pernambuco Baptist Convention showed more books studied and more awards granted there a year or two ago than in any other part of Brazil.

Church architecture, of course, has a direct bearing on religious education. Unless a church building is constructed to meet the educational needs of the members, an adequate program of religious education is hardly possible. Some churches that are being built now—although not all—are giving attention to this vital matter. Churches that have never had a vigorous religious education program find it hard to realize what they have been missing.

The whole field of religious education is receiving larger emphasis and importance than ever before in mission work. Requests for people trained for such a ministry are far more numerous than persons who are equipped to meet the requests.

Justification for theological education anywhere is the example of Jesus. He taught his disciples and also persons who did not belong to that group of twelve. The new believers lacked an adequate understanding of God, Jesus Christ, and God's purpose for man. Christ's aim was to instruct them about God and his ways.

Upon this basis, a program of theological education is an absolute necessity. The people of the world have only an imperfect knowledge of God. If they are to be led to stronger, more adequate faith, their teachers and preachers must be taught the same great truths that Jesus gave to his disciples.

The 1959 *Southern Baptist Convention Annual* reports over three thousand Baptist churches in mission areas with a total membership of more than four hundred thousand. These figures probably reflect fewer churches and members than there actually are. Even though the statistics are admittedly incomplete, they can be studied with other related statistics to ascertain the urgent need for theological education. If complete statistics were available, they, too, would very likely bear out the following conclusions:

1. Most of the ordained nationals in Southern Baptist mission areas are without formal theological training. Efforts to help them increase the effectiveness of their ministry must be intensified.

2. In Southern Baptist mission areas churches outnumber ordained ministers by more than two to one. It is evident, then, that there is a decided dearth of ordained ministers. Young people respond to the call of God in Christian service when they are informed of the need and are given sympathetic guidance. Many leaders are praying that gifted young people in the churches will hear and heed God's call in increasing numbers.

3. The ministry must be made more attractive to promising young men. It should not be necessary for preachers, in order to obtain the recognition they deserve, to practice some other profession in addition to the ministry. Financial support should be sufficient to allow a man with a growing family to think more readily in terms of full-time pastoral leadership or denominational service. Ministers, on the other hand, must seek to merit the dignity and support by securing the best possible preparation for the arduous duties of a full-time ministry.

4. The need for theological education becomes greater as time goes on. In the more than six thousand chapels and mission points in mission areas, services are conducted mainly by devoted laymen, women, and young people. New converts can be

nurtured in the faith up to a certain point by the present leadership. Sooner or later, however, they will need the guidance of God-called pastors who have the very best preparation they can obtain.

The need for a stepped-up program of theological education, therefore, is both evident and insistent. Every seminary and training school, whether national or international, and every theological institute must have faculty reinforcements if more national leaders are to be given the required training.

The late Ruben I. Franks, missionary to Chile, fully understood the importance of the right kind of seminary training. "Though there is an ever-pressing need for more and more missionaries," he said, "still, in these young Chilean men and women who have dedicated their lives to full-time Christian service lies our greatest hope for the evangelization of this country. Adequate seminary training for the national is becoming more and more an important factor in our mission work here."

International seminaries are a fairly recent development in Southern Baptist missions. The first was opened in Europe shortly after World War II. Located in Ruschlikon, in the province of Zurich, Switzerland, it offers theological training of high standard in an international fellowship. The student body usually is made up of approximately forty students from perhaps fifteen European countries.

The other two international seminaries are maintained in Spanish America, one in Buenos Aires, Argentina, and the other in Cali, Colombia. The Buenos Aires seminary expects an enrolment of one hundred in the very near future. The Cali seminary is not so far along in its development, but the student body is growing, the physical equipment is becoming much more adequate, and its international aspect is being greatly enhanced.

Although it is considered among national schools, the seminary located at Baguio, in the Philippines, also has an international flavor in that it has both English-language and Chinese-language divisions. This seminary in the Philippines and others in new missions in the Orient give evidence of the value that is placed now on leadership training.

Most of the older missions were in existence for years before seminaries were established. Baptist seminaries were established in the Philippines, Indonesia, Malaya, Thailand, Taiwan, Hong Kong, and Korea within a few years after the first missionaries (most of whom transferred from China following its occupation by Communists) entered those countries.

The theological seminary in Ogbomosho, Nigeria, by meeting academic standards set by the Southern Baptist Theological Seminary in Kentucky, graduates its students with degrees from the American institution. The West African seminary has a large student body of nearly 175. The students preach on the streets of Ogbomosho on Wednesday afternoons. They travel by bicycle as far as twenty-five miles to week-end appointments. Their week-end activities are considered as important to the future effectiveness of young ministers as formal class work.

Each of the seminaries has its own distinctive features. In Yugoslavia, due to a limited student body and a small faculty, pastors come to the seminary from time to time to offer concentrated courses of two weeks' duration. In Spain the Baptist seminary does its work under the watchful eyes of the police.

In Italy the seminary curriculum is designed to fit actual situations in which the students will find themselves as Baptist pastors, and the attempt is also made to prepare the students for graduate study and for service in a land of ancient culture.

Sensing the need for better pre-seminary training, the Italian Baptist seminary has accepted twelve boarding students who live in the dormitory but attend state high schools. The same need is met in various ways in other countries.

At first it was thought that major theological seminaries and training schools in Recife and Rio de Janeiro, Brazil, and in Argentina, Chile, Colombia, and Mexico could minister to Latin America's need for a trained ministry. Experience proved, however, that many students are not prepared scholastically for the work offered by the major institutions, and that some of them need to be identified more closely with Baptist work in their home countries. Consequently, it has seemed wise to establish theological institutions in a number of other countries.

A Hausa Baptist pastors' school is maintained just outside Kaduna, northern Nigeria. Almost one hundred students, both men and women, are enrolled. The fact that the number of Hausa-speaking congregations has increased from about twenty to more than a hundred in just two years is attributed, in large measure, to this school.

A religious education course for girls is offered by the girls' school in Rio. The work is designed to prepare them for training school work, although not all of the girls are able to pursue the training school course. The course offered by the Rio school is of considerable significance because it offers many girls the only training they will ever receive for religious leadership.

Several Baptist seminaries enrol women as well as men. In some countries separate schools are maintained for women. The Armstrong Memorial Training School in Rome, Italy, and the two Brazilian schools in Recife and Rio de Janeiro are well known to most Southern Baptists.

Here and there, correspondence courses in theological subjects are offered for students with families or without sufficient educational background to attempt formal seminary study.

ASSEMBLIES AND ENCAMPMENTS

Assemblies and encampments mean as much in foreign lands as Ridgecrest and Glorieta mean to Southern Baptists in the United States. Amagi Baptist Assembly is already a very vital part of church life in Japan. One thousand or more people attend week-night services at the Jaguaquara encampment in North Brazil.

Israeli Baptists are developing a Baptist center near Petah Tiqva for assembly purposes. In the

Arab world, a mountaintop property has been purchased in Lebanon as a future camp-conference center for Baptists in the Middle East. Italian Baptists have a camp site at Santa Severa, their "Little Ridgecrest-by-the-Sea." Argentina encampments are on both the associational and national levels.

Several of the students who enrolled for the first session in the Peruvian Theological Institute, Lima, surrendered for life service at the Santa Eulalia encampment, which is located in the mountains some thirty miles from the school.

Seminaries are often used for encampments or retreats. The Baptist theological seminary in Switzerland has an elaborate program of summer conferences for pastors, laymen, women, and youth groups.

PUBLICATION WORK

Publication work is the reliable ally of all educational endeavor, whether in schools or churches. The effectiveness of any educational process depends upon several factors. Literature is one of the most important.

"Christian literature brings its message primarily indeed to the individual," says W. H. P. Faunce, "but because the printed page may present the same message at the same time to thousands of readers, it becomes a powerful social and unifying influence."

Publication work requires certain technical abilities. More than that, it requires the ability to look beyond the immediate and personal to ultimate objectives. Miss Mary Lucile Saunders, missionary to the Philippines, where Southern Baptists work in five language areas, puts it this way:

"For those who can look beyond and over and above the confining hours imposed by deadlines and see the wee Beginners, the wriggling Primaries, the fast-growing Juniors, the changing Intermediates, the keen Seniors, the maturing Young People, and the able Adults; for those who are challenged by the power of the written page as well as the spoken word and are willing to sacrifice the personal joy of witnessing person to person for the wider witness through the written page; for such as these, literature work is a marvelous privilege and a challenge to their highest and best."

The Baptist Press, a major publication plant in Hong Kong, provides Baptist literature in Chinese for Taiwan (Formosa) and the overseas Chinese groups in all Southeast Asia, as well as for Hong Kong and Macao. It has published a Chinese Bible in an edition of twenty thousand copies. Five other publication centers serve the literature needs of Baptists in the Orient. One of them, the Jordan Press in Tokyo, is the publication channel of the Japan Baptist Convention.

Italian Baptists have a new Italian Baptist Publishing House. The influence of evangelical literature in a Catholic country can hardly be overstated. Mrs. Roy Starmer writes, "In a land where it is a sin even to enter an evangelical church, evangelical literature is of supreme importance. Although it is difficult to get Catholic people to attend our churches, they will read our publications."

Nigeria has a large publication center in Ibadan. In Central Africa, however, the missionaries have had to shoulder extra loads in order to supply the literature they must have. Almost all members of the mission there share in the publication program on an assignment basis.

The Baptist Spanish Publishing House, El Paso, Texas, serves approximately one hundred thousand Spanish-speaking Baptists in forty countries. Its staff has undertaken in recent years to help solve a perennial problem in theological education—lack of suitable textbooks. Eleven texts, including a Hebrew grammar, either have been published and released or are in process of production. A new unified study course for churches has been introduced by the Publishing House. The course provides diplomas by departments and combines Sunday school and Training Union studies in the same course.

Southern Baptists who attend the Baptist World Alliance Congress in Rio de Janeiro, Brazil, in 1960, will see their largest publication enterprise anywhere in the world. The remarkable progress made by Brazilian Baptists is linked inseparably to the Carroll Publishing House and its work. A steady stream of books, quarterlies, and tracts flows from its presses to churches and book stores in all parts of Brazil.

The Bible Press, which is operated in connection with the Publishing House in Rio, is without a parallel anywhere in our mission operations. At the present time Brazil is second only to the United States in the distribution of Bibles and Scripture portions, and this is due in part to the expanding program of the Bible Press.

It has conducted a unique campaign to get every Christian to give away or sell at least one Bible during the year. One church responded by sending forty people out on bicycles Sunday after Sunday to carry Bibles to every house in the city and the surrounding countryside. Organized in 1942, over a million copies of the Scriptures in Portuguese have been produced by the Bible Press.

Santiago, Chile, is the base for an international program of Woman's Missionary Union publications in the Spanish language.

One of the major denominational enterprises of Argentine Baptists is its publication board. In addition to carrying on its own publication program, it distributes the splendid publications of the El Paso Publishing House.

Baptist groups now thrive in countries where the first knowledge of Baptists and what they stand for was introduced, not by missionaries, pastors, or church members, but by literature from some Baptist publication center.

Christian education—whether it is given through publications, schools, or churches—is an integral part of Christian missions. Many of the world's people have secured their education without being brought to a knowledge of the truth as it is in Jesus. God intended for man to learn, but he also expected him to learn the right things.

People may disagree about how well educated men like Hitler, Marx, and Lenin were, but none can deny that they used their minds very effectively to influence the world. It is futile to conjecture about what their influence might have been if they had been Christians; the practical reality confronting the world is that they were not. Some of the world's gravest problems and most agonizing frustrations are due to that.

Men's minds are in quest of knowledge. If the right kind is not made available, the wrong kind comes in to fill the vacuum. Herein lies the insistent opportunity for Christian education. It fulfils its highest destiny by making possible "Evangelism Through Teaching." By this means also Christ's kingdom comes!

4

Evangelism Through Healing

"THE ministry of health and healing belongs to the essence of the Gospel and is, therefore, an integral part of the mission to which Christ has called, and is calling, His Church."[1]

This statement, adopted by representatives of all the major Christian missionary agencies at an international missionary conference in Madras, India, in 1938, has not been seriously challenged from that day to this. It represents the considered judgment of most thoughtful Christians.

The Christian ministry of healing is not an afterthought, not an extra that can be dispensed with at will. It "belongs to the essence of the Gospel." Medical missions is not an appendage to the missionary enterprise; it is "an integral part of the mission to which Christ has called, and is calling, His Church."

Medical missions is a means of evangelism, a way of witnessing that flows naturally and inevitably from the very nature of the gospel of redeeming love.

It was not always possible to make such a statement as that made at Madras and expect it to be

[1] *The Life of the Church,* Vol. IV, "Madras Series," International Missionary Council, New York, 1939, p. 163.

accepted without argument. Medical mission service passed through a long period in which it was forced to demonstrate its value, to win its right to exist. It is strange that this should have been so, but it has.

That medical missions should have been slow in gaining recognition is especially strange because the very first Protestant missionary of modern times was a medical doctor. Before William Carey was appointed by the Baptist Missionary Society of England in 1793, a doctor named John Thomas had already been designated a missionary to India. Carey was appointed to go with Dr. Thomas, who had already been in India as a ship's surgeon in the employ of the British East India Company. The British physician was familiar with conditions in India and desired to return, not as a medical doctor for the British colonists, but as a minister of the gospel to the people of India.

While Dr. Thomas did not go to India specifically for the purpose of practicing medicine, the very first convert won by the two missionaries came largely as a result of the medical ministry of the doctor. A Hindu man named Krishna Pal came to Dr. Thomas with an ailment which responded to treatment. While he treated the patient, Dr. Thomas witnessed to him, and Krishna Pal continued to come for instruction after his recovery. On Christmas Day, 1800, William Carey baptized him, the first convert after seven years of almost fruitless missionary labor in India. The point of contact had been the medical ministry of Dr. Thomas.

This beginning was symbolic and prophetic. Again and again, medical missions have been the means of overcoming barriers, breaking down prejudices, winning a hearing for the gospel. Many a heart has been opened "at the point of the lancet." Many a resistant mission field has been opened by means of medical missions.

Despite the experience of Dr. Thomas, it was nearly a hundred years before medical missions gained recognition. Not until 1894 did the Baptist Missionary Society appoint a medical doctor with the specific purpose of beginning a program of medical work in India.[2] Several men with medical training had been appointed previously, but they had full theological training and went out primarily as preachers. Medical work was a side line.

Other denominations had pioneered in medical missions before Baptists made a beginning. The Dutch Reformed Church sent Dr. John Scudder to India in 1819. The Congregational Church sponsored Dr. Peter Parker in China in 1835. Dr. David Livingstone went to Africa in 1840 under the London Missionary Society. In 1884 Dr. H. N. Allen, a Presbyterian physician, gained entrance to Korea when the country was tightly closed to all missionaries and, through the influence of his medical skill, was able to gain admittance for his missionary colleagues.

Despite the obvious effectiveness of early medical missions, as late as 1900 many conservative Christians regarded this as a questionable innovation.

[2] Townley Lord, *Achievement*, p. 85.

"Missionaries are not to heal men's bodies, but to save their souls," was a position commonly stated. Medical missions had yet to prove its right to exist.

THE EXAMPLE OF JESUS

Resistance to the concept of medical missions seems strange, not only in the light of their effectiveness, but in the light of the Bible itself. The healing ministry of Jesus is one of the most prominent features of his life as recorded in the Gospels.

At the very beginning of his ministry in his home town of Nazareth Jesus announced, by reading from the prophet Isaiah, the purpose for which God had sent him: "The Spirit of the Lord is upon me, because he hath anointed me to preach the gospel to the poor; he hath sent me to heal the brokenhearted, to preach deliverance to the captives, and recovering of sight to the blind, to set at liberty them that are bruised, to preach the acceptable year of the Lord" (Luke 4:18-19 as quoted from Isa. 61:1).

A graphic description of the ministry of Jesus is given in Matthew 4:23,24: "And Jesus went about all Galilee, teaching in their synagogues, and preaching the gospel of the kingdom, and healing all manner of sickness and all manner of disease among the people. And his fame went throughout all Syria: and they brought unto him all sick people that were taken with divers diseases and torments, and those which were possessed with devils, and those which were lunatick, and those that had the palsy; and he healed them."

Preaching, teaching, and healing were the three

unfailing and inseparable elements of the ministry of Jesus wherever he went. He preached because he had good news to proclaim. He taught because he had truth to convey. He healed because his compassionate heart went out to suffering humanity.

Jesus did not perform miracles of healing merely to attract crowds so that he might preach to them. He did not withhold his healing mercies from those who did not recognize fully who he was and accept his claims upon them. He healed as a natural, spontaneous expression of his love for men and his desire to see them made whole. He healed to demonstrate God's power and to reveal his own divine compassion.

Jesus not only engaged in an intensive ministry of healing himself, he also commanded his disciples to heal. When the twelve were sent on their first missionary journey they were instructed to preach, but they were also instructed to heal. Their Master told them: "And as ye go, preach, saying, The kingdom of heaven is at hand. Heal the sick, cleanse the lepers, raise the dead, cast out devils: freely ye have received, freely give" (Matt. 10:7,8).

When the seventy were sent out later, Jesus' instructions to them included the words: "And into whatsoever city ye enter, and they receive you, eat such things as are set before you: And heal the sick that are therein, and say unto them, The kingdom of God is come nigh unto you" (Luke 10:8,9).

The book of Acts indicates that healing played an important part in the process by which Christianity spread throughout the apostolic period. The disciples continued the work of preaching, teaching, and healing wherever they went. Men and women believed the gospel not only because its truth appealed to their minds, but also because they beheld the revelation of God's power and the demonstration that he was a God of love who was concerned with diseased bodies as well as with rebellious wills and immortal souls.

Miracles began to decline toward the end of the apostolic age. Healing wrought by Christians came more and more through normal processes, in response to a ministry of devoted care to the suffering rather than in response to instantaneous acts of miraculous power. But the church, when it has been true to its Founder, has never been able to neglect the ministry of healing.

Wherever evangelical Christian faith has gone, it has made a difference in the lives of men, even as it made a difference in their eternal destiny. It has brought release to captives, sight to the blind, healing to the brokenhearted. And it has been when this demonstration of God's power through the lives of his witnesses has revealed that he cares for the bodies of men as well as their souls, that men have been most ready to believe that God so loved them as to send his only Son to redeem them.

It would be a mistake to try to reproduce the miracles of the New Testament in order to obey literally the words of Jesus to "heal the sick." But miracles of healing are possible today through modern medicine. God has guided the minds of men into the discovery of wonderful things about the human body. He expects us to use the things we have learned.

Healing is nonetheless wonderful because modern surgery makes it possible, or because one of the "miracle drugs" is employed. The miraculous element seems less only because we think we understand the physical laws which operate to make healing possible. Even the doctor does not fully understand how healing takes place; he can only stand in awe as the Great Physician does his work, Modern medicine, reverently employed, is one of the best demonstrations of love in action.

Medical missions belongs to the very essence of the missionary enterprise. It is a means of evangelism; a way of witnessing to the love of God as revealed in Jesus Christ; a method of confronting men with God's mighty acts, and with his supreme act of self-revelation in the living Christ.

SOUTHERN BAPTIST MEDICAL MISSIONS

The first regularly appointed medical missionary sent out by the Foreign Mission Board of the Southern Baptist Convention was Dr. T. W. Ayers, who went to China in 1900. Although he was appointed partly to take care of the needs of missionaries in China, he soon gave most of his time to a medical ministry to the Chinese. He found that it was not only a work of mercy, but a means of Christian witness.

An influential Chinese man once witnessed an operation that Dr. Ayers performed. When he learned from the doctor's language teacher that the foreigner had come ten thousand miles to heal the suffering people of China with no expectation of money from them, he said to the Christian Chinese teacher:

"I have heard you on the streets tell the story of your Jesus, but what you said went in at one ear and out at the other. Today I have seen something with my eyes, and there is no opening in the back of my head for it to go out. I must confess to you that your Jesus religion is the only religion in the world that has ever sent a man forth to act as we have seen it here today." [3]

Within twenty years, Southern Baptists were operating hospitals in eight strategic cities of China. For many years missionary doctors and nurses, assisted by trained Chinese workers, carried on a ministry of mercy in these eight centers. No one will ever know how much the Chinese were influenced to follow Christ because of the witness of the Christian hospitals.

When the Communists overran China in 1949, most American missionaries began to leave because it was all but impossible to carry on their work under the Communist regime. Dr. William L. Wallace, a bachelor physician stationed at Wuchow hospital, elected to remain. Nurse Everley Hayes remained to help him.

False charges were brought against the doctor and he was thrown into a Communist prison. Subjected to countless indignities, he remained unwavering in

[3] E. C. Routh, *Evening and Morning in China* (Nashville: Broadman Press, 1950), p. 86.

his commitment to Christian truth and his avowal that he was in China only to serve the Chinese people. At last he was put to death by brutal authorities, who tried to make it appear that he had committed suicide.

Everley Hayes survived to witness his funeral and after a few months was allowed to leave China, bringing an end to a glorious chapter in Southern Baptist medical missions. All of the Baptist hospitals in China have either been taken over by the government or are being operated under conditions in which Christian witnessing is all but impossible.

One of the medical missionaries who had worked in China before the Communists closed the door was Dr. N. A. Bryan. Unable to return to China, he went to Pusan, Korea, in 1951 and opened a small clinic in a tent. Other missionaries joined him. At the height of the Korean conflict, he and his helpers treated over seven hundred patients each day. Early in 1956 a hospital was opened, fittingly called William L. Wallace Memorial Baptist Hospital. Other hospitals opened in the Orient by Southern Baptist missionaries are located in the Philippines at Mati on the island of Mindanao, in Japan at Kyoto, and in Indonesia at Kediri on the island of Java.

A missionary doctor, George Green, was first appointed to Nigeria in 1907. Although a medical doctor, he was also a preacher, and in his early years had little opportunity for medical work. In 1911 he opened a small dispensary, but not until 1923 were funds made available for a real hospital building at Ogbomosho. Hospitals were established later at Shaki, Joinkrama, and Eku, three widely separated towns. Since the withdrawal of missionaries from China, Southern Baptists have had a greater concentration of medical work in Nigeria than in any other country.

Hospitals have been established more recently in three African countries other than Nigeria. In 1953 a 44-bed hospital was opened at Sanyati in Southern Rhodesia; in 1958 a 14-bed hospital was opened at Nalerigu in northern Ghana; in 1959 a 104-bed tuberculosis hospital was established at Mbeya in Tanganyika.

Three mission hospitals have been established by Southern Baptists in Latin America. Early efforts to establish medical missions in Mexico were disrupted by revolutions. A new beginning was made in 1947 when missionary doctors were sent to Mexico, Paraguay, and Colombia. The forty-bed hospital in Asuncion, Paraguay, opened in 1952; the fifty-bed hospital in Barranquilla, Colombia, in 1954; the fifty-bed hospital in Guadalajara, Mexico, in 1958. Medical regulations in the Latin American countries require foreign doctors to take national medical examinations in the national language and to qualify in other ways that vary from country to country.

Medical missions have long been recognized as a strategic means of witnessing in the Near East because open evangelism is prohibited by law in most of the Moslem countries. Even educational missions cannot be carried on without restrictions. But medical services are so greatly needed that the Arab countries will often permit doctors and nurses to enter when other missionaries would not be permitted.

In 1952 Southern Baptists took over the operation of a forty-bed hospital located in Ajloun, Jordan. It had been founded by an independent British doctor who, facing the time of retirement, offered it to the Foreign Mission Board, which paid him for the buildings and took over the project. In 1954 the Board assumed the operation of a ninety-two-bed hospital in the Gaza Strip, between Egypt and the new nation of Israel. This hospital had been operated for eighty years by the Church Missionary Society of Britain, which was forced to relinquish it because of anti-British sentiment and lack of financial support.

The Foreign Mission Board now (as of June, 1959) operates 18 hospitals in 13 countries. Forty-six missionary doctors work in co-operation with 55 national physicians. They are assisted by 54 missionary nurses and 187 national nurses. Other personnel on the staff of Baptist hospitals overseas include 19 missionaries serving as medical technicians, hospital administrators, chaplains, or in other capacities, and over 300 national employees of various grades. There are also 62 clinics and dispensaries, some of which are served by the medical staff attached to one of the hospitals. Seven countries which have no Baptist hospital (Brazil, Chile, Ecuador, Taiwan, Hong Kong, Malaya, and Italy) have Baptist clinics. About 250,000 patients a year are treated at the Baptist medical centers.

MEDICAL EVANGELISM

Medical missions are, as has been said, a way of witnessing, a means of evangelism. How is this witness borne? What methods are used to make medical service an effective evangelizing agency? Let us look first at the typical mission hospital, and then take note of clinics, dispensaries, leprosy colonies, and other types of community service which can lead men into a living relationship with Christ.

First let it be noted that a Baptist hospital gives a silent witness just by being there. It *says something* to all who pass by, even though they never enter its doors. They are bound to ask, "What are those buildings? Who put them there? Why?" The Baptist hospital building says that somebody cares and keeps on saying it day and night, year in and year out.

Doctors and nurses also bear a silent witness through their acts of loving service. It is true that "actions speak louder than words." When a perspiring surgeon toils with skilled hands over the operating table, he is saying, without words, something concerning his love for the patient. When a nurse changes bandages on festering wounds, empties bedpans, or answers an emergency call at midnight, she is saying something about Christian love more convincingly than she could say it with any number of words.

And yet, words are necessary, too. Actions must be explained in clear and simple terms so that there will be no mistaking the motive behind them. Fewer words are needed when they accompany action, and they are given an eloquence that would be lacking were they not backed up by deeds of kindness. But "faith cometh by hearing, and hearing by the word of God" (Rom. 10:17). In addition to performing acts of loving service, the medical missionary must speak words of testimony if the patient is to hear and respond in faith. The combination of spoken word and eloquent action provides a witness of unusual effectiveness.

In most mission hospitals, the work of evangelization begins before the patient is ever admitted. Hospitals always minister to a large number of outpatients—persons who do not require major surgery and can return to their homes immediately after treatment. Since the people usually begin gathering long before the time appointed for treatment, the waiting room for outpatients makes an ideal place for a religious service. People are there with time on their hands, and they feel a very definite need for help.

In almost every mission hospital a brief preaching service is held daily for the outpatients. Sometimes it is conducted by one of the doctors; but more often it is a responsibility of someone else—another missionary or a national pastor who serves as chaplain of the hospital. A gospel message heard while waiting to see the doctor is the first contact that many a patient has with the Christian faith. Although the messages are often evangelistic, an invitation usually is not given because many of the outpatients do not have sufficient background to make an intelligent, definite decision. But a beginning is made when the patients are led to think about their relationship to God.

Following the religious service, the clinic for outpatients begins. They are called one at a time for examination and treatment. Leaving the waiting room, each goes first to a registration desk, where a trained worker records on the hospital's entrance cards his name, age, address, previous record of treatments, and his religious affiliation. The registrar may be one of the nurses, the wife of a missionary doctor, or a trained national worker.

Although the time given to each patient must be brief because the line is long, the Christian worker has an opportunity to speak a few well-chosen words as each answers questions about his religious beliefs. Furthermore, the registration record provides the information for evangelistic work after the patient returns to his home. Many excellent prospects for evangelism are found among hospital record cards. The opportunities for fruitful follow-up work usually are limited only by lack of personnel to make the necessary visits.

Outpatients come to the hospital, hear a Christian message while waiting, receive treatment, and go home. Unless there is a follow-up visit, the contact is brief and the evangelistic opportunity limited. However, the same patient often returns repeatedly for treatment, and over a period of time he may be won to Christ through the service at the hospital.

There is greater opportunity with patients who, because they need surgery or prolonged treatment, are admitted to the hospital as bed patients. The length of their stay averages about one week in most places. The number of inpatients is limited, of course, by the capacity of the hospital.

Two definite types of evangelistic ministry are carried on among inpatients in mission hospitals: services in the wards and a personal bedside ministry. A typical mission hospital might be described as having three or four wards with from ten to twenty beds in each. The beds are nearly always filled with patients awaiting surgery, recovering from surgery, or receiving other types of treatment. A daily service is almost always conducted in each ward, the preacher being a missionary, a hospital chaplain, or a local pastor.

A patient usually is grateful to the hospital staff for its service to him. Often he is conscious that his life has been saved by what the doctors and nurses have done for him. Having come face to face with the serious issues of life and death, he is psychologically prepared to face his need for a Saviour and to make a grateful response to the grace of God as it is made known to him.

There are problems connected with ward services. Some of the patients are too sick to listen to a sermon. It is difficult sometimes to stop the busy routine long enough to have a quiet service. Always there is danger that the staff may become so engrossed with necessary medical duties that the hospital's spiritual ministry is neglected. The danger becomes even more acute in hospitals where inadequate facilities cause overcrowding, and where staff members are seriously overworked because of insufficient personnel. But the missionary staff knows the necessity of keeping the evangelistic ministry central in the life of the hospital and works toward that aim.

At a Baptist hospital in West Africa, the problem of a time for religious services has been solved by establishing a regular time for simultaneous services. "Every morning at 10:30 all work stops at the Baptist hospital in Ogbomosho, Nigeria," says Nurse Antonina Canzoneri, Southern Baptist missionary, "and the gospel is preached throughout the hospital—in all the wards, in the clinics, and in the waiting rooms. Different staff members are assigned to preach in different stations each day."[4] In some hospitals, a chaplain goes from ward to ward and holds a service in each.

While ward services are valuable assets, the heart of hospital evangelism is the intensely individual and personal bedside witness of doctors, nurses, chaplains, and others. There is often a cumulative effect when different members of the hospital staff speak a cheery word, pause for a moment of prayer, sit at the bedside to read the Bible, tarry to discuss the patient's personal problems or to hear his confession of faith.

For the individual patient, this chain of witnessing may begin while the nurse is preparing him for the operating room. She may calm his fears, speak a word of encouragement, quote a verse of Scripture, or breathe a brief prayer.

[4] "Healing the Sin-Sick," *The Commission*, March, 1959, p. 5.

The surgeon and his assistants in the operating room always pause for a moment of prayer before beginning an operation. Usually, the surgeon himself leads this prayer, humbly asking the Great Physician to guide his hands and to heighten his skill, and committing the patient into the keeping of a gracious God. If the patient speaks a dialect that the doctor is unable to use, the prayer may be led by one of the nurses or orderlies who can speak the patient's language so that he may be directly blessed by the prayer and realize the dependence of the medical staff upon divine guidance.

The period of convalescence following an operation presents an ideal time for personal evangelism on the part of the doctor. As he visits his patients in the wards, prescribing their postoperative care, the missionary surgeon almost always pauses by each bedside to speak a personal word.

To the patient who realizes that the skilled physician has turned his back upon a remunerative practice in America to minister to people in greater need, this simple word carries great weight. Many times the patient is aware that he owes his life to the doctor. These circumstances make an ideal occasion for the doctor to explain the simple plan of salvation and to point the patient to the One to whom he owes, not only life itself, but redemption and life everlasting.

Sometimes there is an immediate response to the bedside ministry of a medical missionary. In some cases, one person can be said to be directly responsible for winning a person to a saving knowledge of

Christ. More often it is a combination of the ward services and the personal witness of several different persons. Pauline Jackson, missionary nurse at the Baptist hospital on the Sanyati Reserve in Southern Rhodesia, tells a touching story of how the combined efforts of the entire hospital staff resulted in winning a family to Christ:

"Emelia, a frightened young girl, came to our hospital to await the birth of her baby. Because she had lost a baby the year before at her home, we at the hospital worked and prayed especially hard, trusting that she would have a live, healthy child. The baby was born—not a fine, big baby, but a beautiful little girl weighing three and a half pounds.

"While in the hospital, Emelia talked with the missionaries and heard the sermons in the daily chapel service. Our eyes met one day when the invitation to accept Christ was given at the close of a service. Misery and yearning were plain in hers; and she seemed only to need the encouragement she received when I smiled and nodded yes. Emelia got up and went to the front of the group, making public her decision for Christ.

"From that time on it was a race to see who was growing the faster—the baby or her mother. As we weighed the little premature child and rejoiced over each ounce she gained, we watched Emelia grow in her trust and love for Christ. The nurses helped her memorize Bible verses, as she could not read. In this way she could share the verses with those in her village when she returned home.

"Finally, the baby was large enough to go home.

Up until that time she had been known as Baby Emelia. Now her mother wanted us to give her a name. We had a special service for this purpose. The name we chose was Tendai, the Shona word for 'trust ye' or 'believe ye.' This is the same word that is used in Acts 16:31 when it says, 'Believe on the Lord Jesus Christ.' In the service we read that verse and explained what it means. Then we told how we hoped others would be led to trust in Christ when they heard the name of the baby. After the prayer of dedication for Tendai, mother and daughter started on their long journey home.

"The rains came and we heard no more from Emelia and Tendai. How often I thought of them and realized that if they were sick they would not be able to come for help because of an impassable river. Then, one day after the rains, my heart rejoiced as I saw Emelia coming up the road in front of my house with Tendai tied on her back. She told me that her husband was beginning work on our mission station as a brickmaker.

"After that I saw them frequently as she worked with her husband at the brickkiln, and then several times when Tendai was very sick and in our hospital. One day I heard of the conversion of the father." [5]

Medical evangelism is not easy. Sometimes it takes the persistent efforts of the entire medical staff, plus earnest follow-up work, to bring about a conversion. Dr. Karl J. Myers of the Baptist hospital in Ogbomosho, Nigeria, relates such an incident:

[5] Pauline Jackson, "Tendai—More Than a Name," *The Commission,* March, 1959, p. 20.

"A little more than a year ago a three-year-old child and his mother were admitted to the hospital in Ogbomosho, both with tuberculosis. The little boy Lasisi, was nearly dead. His lungs were so diseased that for a whole month he could only pant, but gradually he became better. We talked to his mother each day and the nurses read to her from the Bible. She said she would like to become a Christian but would do so only if her husband would consent.

"When her husband came we said to him: 'How thankful we are to God that your son is nearly well. Because God has shown his love to us, we share his love for your son.' I started to quote John 3:16 and he, a Moslem, finished it! He knew it as well as I. I thought, 'God has not left us to work alone; others, under his guidance, often pave the way for us.' The man joined me in prayer that his wife and child might be healed and that he might know the truth.

"That this prayer might be answered, Pastor Ogunyale and I drove to the man's village one evening. We got stuck in the mud; and, after working an hour without freeing the car, we walked the rest of the way to the town through the darkness. I decided that perhaps the Lord doesn't always pave the way so smoothly after all.

"We found the family and learned that the father was the town's *Balogun*, or 'general of the army' (a purely honorary position in a town of a thousand people). He got some men to help us. Then, while we walked back to the car, he told us that he and his wife had decided to become Christians but that they needed much help. They came to our school for converts last winter. Since that time we have visited them each month, taking with us the pastor and some deacons from the closest Baptist church, three miles away.

"On one visit last spring we found Lasisi's entire body covered with pustules. He was recovering from smallpox. We returned to vaccinate the rest of the townspeople, and then we met with his family to thank God that Lasisi had survived a second deadly illness. We asked the *Balogun* if he would like to pray.

"His prayer, though still voiced in the Moslem fashion of repeating each phrase, was one of thanks to Christ for his son's recovery. He says he cannot help but see the Lord's hand in all of the things that have happened to him this year, since he first got courage enough to take his child to our hospital instead of to a Moslem priest or an Ifa medicine man for treatment." [6]

One of the difficulties of medical evangelism is due to the limited time available for influencing patients. For the first few days after an operation, the patient is usually too sick to receive much value from a bedside witness. After a few days of convalescence, he is dismissed; and any interest awakened while he was in the hospital may die unless there is some definite follow-up.

In many cases the time in the hospital has not been sufficient to awaken interest, give instruction,

[6] "Epistles from Today's Apostles All over the World," *The Commission*, November, 1958, pp. 22, 23.

bring about a decision, and allow enough Christian growth to assure continuation of the Christian life. This problem should largely be solved at the Baptist tuberculosis hospital which has just been opened in Mbeya, Tanganyika. It is estimated that the average length of stay there will be not one week, but from six weeks to two months.

Until the recent development of sulfone-type drugs, tuberculosis patients required complete rest and continuous treatment for several years. By means of these new drugs, the average case can be completely arrested now and the patient may be discharged as fully cured within about six weeks. During that period, the patient is usually not very sick. He can listen to a sermon and unless his case is very serious, join in a song service. If he is literate, he is able to sit up and read. Six weeks in a Christian atmosphere, with daily ward services, constant personal witnessing from the staff, opportunities to read the Bible and Christian literature, time to think, pray, and grow, should provide an ideal situation in which evangelism can be carried on in the Mbeya tuberculosis hospital.

On the other hand, the 104 beds will not be tied up indefinitely by the same patients. There will be a complete turnover in personnel among the patients about every two months, which means that each year approximately six hundred persons will pass through the hospital, receive treatment, remain long enough to hear the gospel repeatedly, and then move on to make room for others.

The hospital has not been in operation long

enough to observe the results, but many lasting conversions are anticipated from the evangelistic ministry of the hospital. Eventually, churches may spring up all over Tanganyika because of patients who have recovered and returned to their native villages to bear witness concerning what great things God has done for them.

A field of evangelism in mission hospitals of which few people are aware is within the hospital staff itself. The ideal is to have an all-Christian staff, and this ideal has been attained by the Japan Baptist Hospital in Kyoto, which takes justifiable pride in the fact that, although the country is dominantly Buddhist, its staff is 100 per cent Christian.

Not all mission hospitals are so fortunate, for it is sometimes impossible to secure enough Christian doctors and nurses to operate a large hospital. (We are familiar with the fact that not every physician on the staff of a Baptist hospital in the United States is necessarily a Baptist; and not all the nurses on the staff of a Baptist hospital in this country are devoted church members.)

This emphasizes the importance of the daily chapel service for the hospital staff. It is held at a noonday period or early in the morning before the day's work begins and usually is entirely separate from the services held for hospital patients. In most cases, all doctors, interns, nurses, and other hospital employees who can get away from floor duty attend. For Christians, the service is a time of inspiration and renewal of spiritual strength. It tones up the spiritual life and sends the staff back to the wards with a feeling of inner strength and a more radiant witness.

The chapel services present an opportunity for evangelization of non-Christians who may be on the hospital staff. Student nurses who came to the hospital only because it offered an opportunity to learn a vocation and secure employment have found Christ while they were in nursing school and have committed themselves to a life of medical service, not as a way of making a living, but as a means of expressing Christian love.

A remarkable instance of successful evangelism within the hospital staff came about at the Baptist hospital in Ajloun, Jordan. It has been necessary in the past to employ some staff members who were either Moslem or from Orthodox, Armenian, or Catholic background. Missionary William O. Hern who is in charge of evangelism on the Ajloun station writes:

"Every young man who lives on the mission compound has made some kind of an outward profession of faith in Christ as Saviour. We feel that most of them are really converted. Every nurse and nursing student has also made a profession of faith in Christ." [7]

It is obvious that when members of the hospital staff are converted, they in turn can witness to the patients, and the evangelistic process goes on in widening circles.

[7] Minutes of Arab Baptist Mission, July 14-17, 1958, p. 16.

CLINICS OR DISPENSARIES

In seventeen different countries, Southern Baptists operate more than sixty medical centers that are not called hospitals, but "clinics," "dispensaries," "welfare centers," or some other name. Sometimes it is difficult to distinguish between a hospital and a clinic.

In general, a medical center is called a hospital only if it has at least one qualified medical doctor giving his full time to the center and if it makes provision for inpatients as well as outpatients.

The clinic or dispensary may be a treatment center in charge of a trained nurse and visited only occasionally by a doctor. In most cases, having no beds, it is equipped only to take care of outpatients. A clinic may be almost as busy as a regular hospital. Some dispensaries provide every type of treatment except major surgery.

The Hong Kong Baptist Clinic, which was opened January 2, 1956, in a second floor apartment in the heart of the city of Kowloon, proved to be a hospital in embryo. One hundred and six patients visited the clinic the first month. Before the end of the year, nearly one thousand were being treated each month. In the second year the number went up to about two thousand patients a month. In 1958 an adjoining flat was purchased to help take care of the crowds. More recently, the government granted a large plot of land for an eighty-bed hospital adjacent to the Baptist college.

The Ire Welfare Center in Nigeria is a maternity

clinic. Founded years ago as a dispensary and treatment center, it has been developed by Miss Eva Sanders and Miss Helen Masters into one of the busiest obstetrical stations in the country. In 1957, babies delivered at the Ire Welfare Center numbered 899, more than in many of the hospitals. A midwifery school has been established there, where African girls learn to deliver babies in a safe and sanitary manner. Gradually they will replace the midwives who use crude and painful methods and often lose both mother and baby. The thirty-six girls enrolled in the midwifery school receive excellent training in Bible as well as in science.

In several of the Latin American countries where Southern Baptists have no medical missionaries, free Baptist clinics are operated by national doctors and nurses. These are often located in areas where they can serve underprivileged people. An example is the Everett Gill, Jr., Memorial Clinic, in Fortaleza, Brazil. Dedicated in the fall of 1956, it is named in honor of a former Foreign Mission Board secretary for Latin America. It was started by Dr. Silas Munguba, a distinguished young surgeon, son of one of Brazil's outstanding Baptist pastors, himself a deacon in the First Baptist Church of Fortaleza. Assisting him are Miss Merces Parente and Dr. Edil Romalho, also a Baptist and son of a Brazilian pastor.

An article in *The Commission* (September, 1958, p. 7), describes the clinic:

"At first the clinic occupied a rented building in a poor suburb where the need was great. But Catholic influence caused the people to prefer sickness to contact with Baptists. After going to another poor suburb, the clinic again met conditions which made it advisable to move.

"This time a site was chosen in the center of the city where the rush and bustle make it possible for a person to visit the clinic without the knowledge of his neighbors. A very large room was divided into a suite, and the clinic reopened bearing Dr. Gill's name.

"Since then the waiting room has been filled with the sick and weary. Hundreds of operations have been performed, babies have been delivered, and many other people have been helped in other ways.

"In the waiting room are copies of the national Baptist paper and other denominational literature, as well as the Portuguese *Reader's Digest*. As the patients leave the clinic, Miss Parente gives them tracts and Gospels. In a file by her desk she keeps a record of the spiritual and physical history of each patient.

"Most of them are Catholics who have not forgotten that they are forbidden to go to the Baptist clinic, even in search of health. The living room atmosphere helps put them at ease as they wait for the doctor to examine them."

A Baptist dispensary at Okuta, Nigeria, is in charge of Mrs. Archie Dunaway, a missionary who is a trained nurse. Her husband, a field missionary, has general supervision of several small churches in the Okuta area, which is largely pagan. The dispensary is a simple two-room building. Its front door opens into a small waiting room furnished with several crude wooden benches. Behind the waiting room is the treatment room.

On mornings when the dispensary is open, Mr. Dunaway tries to arrange his schedule so that he can stay at home with the children while Mrs. Dunaway works at the dispensary. The waiting patients crowd the small waiting room, sitting on the benches and standing around the walls and in the door. Mrs. Dunaway reads the Scriptures to them and talks briefly of what she has read. Then she goes into the treatment room and, with the assistance of trained African helpers, examines babies, gives injections, bandages wounds, and treats ugly tropical ulcers. More serious cases are taken to the Shaki Baptist Hospital, which is about forty miles away. Many hear the gospel for the first time at the dispensary.

The Baptist dispensary at Iwo, Nigeria, was established years ago on the campus of Iwo Baptist College to take care of medical needs of the students. It has become a popular treatment center for people from miles around. A resident nurse is in charge. The dispensary has been enlarged, and a few beds are provided for maternity cases. A limited number of inpatients are received.

Missionary Nurse Lolete Dotson tells of a conversion that recently took place at the Iwo dispensary:

"I must tell you about Raimi. He came to us in an extremely weak condition, with iron deficiency anemia. While Raimi was being treated here he had a lot of time to do some serious thinking about his life. College students, dispensary workers, and some of the pastors from town spoke to him; and his seven-year-old boy read the Bible to him.

"Then, one night, he exchanged his Moslem belief for Christianity and found the joy he had been seeking. He sat on the side of his bed, strong again, and said with a radiant smile: 'Nurse, I do not care how much they abuse me back at home. I am a Christian now!'

"Raimi has gone back home. He is still the only Christian in his village, which has no church; but there is hope for the future because one man refuses to give up.

"Two weeks after he left our dispensary, he came back with a list of twenty-five names of people he had spoken to about Christ. 'And,' he added, 'I have taught them all John 3:16.' "[8]

For many years Southern Baptists had only one dental clinic on a mission field. Originally established at Ogbomosho, Nigeria, it was moved several years ago to Ibadan, the largest city in Nigeria. On the second floor of the Baptist Building, near the heart of the city, which is in the Western Region of the country, Dr. H. D. McCamey and Dr. W. W. Logan operated a modern dental office until 1958, when Dr. Logan moved to Enugu to open a new clinic in the capital city of the Eastern Region. In addition to dental work done at the clinics, both dentists visit schools, hospitals, and leprosy settlements.

Dr. McCamey is convinced that dentistry offers an

[8] "Epistles from Today's Apostles All over the World," *The Commission*, April, 1958, p. 22.

ideal opportunity for personal evangelism. "You have them right where you want them," he says with a smile. "They sit there for an hour while you work on their teeth. They can't talk, and they must listen to you. All you have to do is to talk to them about Jesus."

A leprosy colony was established in 1920 on Tai-Kam Island, just off the coast of South China by Dr. John Lake, a Southern Baptist missionary. A devoted work among these unfortunate people, sponsored by the Chinese Baptist Association, was interrupted by the war between China and Japan (1937-1945). Before the colony could be re-established, the Communists forced all missionaries out of China.

In 1930, Dr. B. L. Lockett established a leprosy colony on the outskirts of Ogbomosho, Nigeria. For the past ten years, the Baptist Leprosy Service in Nigeria has been under the direction of Dr. Robert Goldie, and has shown an amazing growth. During the year 1957, 938 inpatients and 419 outpatients were treated at the Ogbomosho settlement. Patients discharged as arrested cases numbered 251.

During the first ten months of 1958, twenty-one patients were baptized into the Lockett Memorial Church at the Ogbomosho colony for leprosy patients, and thirty-nine others joined an inquirers' class.

In addition to the main settlement in Ogbomosho, twenty-three outpatient clinics and nine other settlements are under the supervision of Dr. Goldie.

These are within a radius of 150 miles. African workers are trained to administer treatment, and many of them preach to the patients.

While many leprosy patients are pagan when they enter the settlement, most of those who are discharged leave as Christians. They go back to their native villages to tell their friends and relatives how they have been cleansed of the dread disease and how they have been cleansed also of sin.

In 1958 the Baptist hospital staff at Nalerigu assumed responsibility for leprosy service in a large district in the northern area of Ghana. Dr. George W. Faile is superintendent of the hospital and Dr. Shelby Vance has charge of a circuit of leprosy treatment centers which he visits on a regular schedule. At each center, Dr. Vance preaches to the patients and their friends and relatives before administering treatments. Some of the preaching points developed in connection with leprosy clinics will eventually develop into Baptist churches.

RELATED MINISTRIES

Other forms of service that offer the foreign missionary a point of contact or a demonstration of Christian love, to give more meaning to his words of testimony about Jesus Christ, are children's homes, Good Will Centers, public health projects, and agricultural missions.

Unique among Southern Baptist mission enterprises is the Kersey Children's Home in Nigeria. It was begun thirty years ago by Miss Ruth Kersey, who was then a nurse at the Ogbomosho Baptist hospital. Miss Kersey was touched by the plight of motherless infants. It was commonly believed that when a woman died during childbirth the baby was possessed of a devil, and the little one was abandoned to exposure and certain death. Some Nigerian Christian women dared to defy superstition and rescue a few of the abandoned babies. They brought them to Miss Kersey, who cared for them in her home at first; but as the number of babies increased a suitable building was constructed adjacent to the hospital. The Children's Home grew until it demanded the full time of a missionary nurse. More than seventy babies are cared for each year now.

When they become three or four years of age, homes are found into which they can be adopted. Although they leave the children's home before they are old enough to understand the Christian faith, lasting impressions have been made upon them in the formative years of life. Above all, care for them has given the African community a demonstration of Christian love in action, and has given pagan superstition a telling blow.

The George W. Truett Children's Home in Israel, cares for older children. Established in Nazareth in 1946 to care for children who had lost one or both parents in the bitter fighting between Jews and Arabs, and moved a few years ago to Petah Tiqva, it has provided a haven of refuge for about twenty boys and girls. Many of them are now approaching young manhood and womanhood. One by one, they have come to recognize Jesus as Messiah and

Lord. As they become old enough to leave the home, suitable jobs are found for them. Christian homes will be established in the Jewish state of Israel by some of these young people who have grown up in the George W. Truett Home.

The Italian Baptist Orphanage in Rome was not established by Southern Baptist missionaries, but was founded by the Italian Baptist Convention. Although it is now supported by the Italian Baptists, it has received assistance from mission funds at certain times in the past, and Mrs. Dewey Moore, a missionary, serves as acting director of the orphanage and an adjoining home for old people.

The necessity of these institutions is felt keenly by Italian Baptists, because they do not want their unfortunates to be placed in the prevalent Catholic institutions, where the children would be reared as Catholics, and where Baptist old people would be subjected to discrimination and abuse because of their faith. Already several boys from the orphanage have grown up to become promising young preachers.

A strong Good Will Center program has been developed in Argentina. A well-established center in the city of Rosario enrols over three hundred people in its classes and reaches more than two hundred homes. A new center has recently been opened in Parana, and a number of conversions have been reported there. Three kindergartens are operated in connection with the Good Will Centers. Parents who bring their children to be enrolled in the Baptist kindergarten can often be enlisted in nearby

Baptist churches. Both the kindergartens and the Good Will Centers become agencies for evangelism.

A thriving Good Will Center is located in a crowded tenement section of the city of Tobato, Japan. Working mothers leave their children at its day nursery. Contacts with the parents through the kindergarten sometimes lead to church attendance and conversion.

Two Baptist community centers have been established in East Africa, in the cities of Dar es Salaam (in Tanganyika) and Nairobi (in Kenya). In each case, a modern building has been constructed in a crowded African section. Sewing classes and adult literacy courses are offered for the grownups; recreation, handwork, club activities, and Bible study are offered for children.

Regular Sunday services are held in the community hall, and it is expected that a church will develop in connection with each community center. Africans who probably never would attend a regular church service are attracted by the varied activities of the community center. Disheartened with life in the crowded African quarters of the growing cities, they come in search of life more abundant and find also life everlasting.

Much of the disease and misery in the world is caused by lack of a pure water supply and lack of proper diet. Missionary doctors and nurses usually take the lead in community programs for improvement of these, but they are often reinforced by teachers in mission schools. Classes in physiology, general science, and domestic science provide excellent opportunities for practical instruction in diet and health.

Many diseases of children are due to a lack of protein. African mothers are being taught that, although babies sicken and die on the starchy diet commonly given them, they will flourish on the same food if a handful of black-eyed peas is added each day.

When a simple change in diet can bring dramatic improvement in health and decrease in disease, it is imperative to teach people in certain parts of the world how to produce the foods their bodies need. Missionary Robert Parham, who has a degree in agriculture, is developing in Nigeria a program that has as its aim the introduction of certain basic foods now absent from the usual diet there, but producible by the African farmer.

The program of instruction, for which the agricultural missionary and a medical doctor form a team, is to be centered in the Baptist churches and carried out into the homes and farms of the people. The person who can show men the way to raise better crops and to have healthier bodies will be given a respectful hearing when he tells them the way that leads to life eternal.

Jesus said, "I am come that they might have life, and that they might have it more abundantly" (John 10:10*b*). The abundant life which he came to bestow includes physical, social, moral, and spiritual elements. He made no distinctions between a man's body, his mind, and his soul. He ministered to the whole man.

He fed the hungry multitudes; he healed the sick; he caused the lame to walk; he illumined the darkened minds of men; he straightened out their perverted wills; he led them to give themselves in glad surrender to the will of God. Having fed them, he taught them to understand that man lives not by bread alone, but by every word that proceeds out of the mouth of God. He brought life abundant here and life eternal hereafter. The two were often wrapped in the same package, and the faith that brought healing brought also forgiveness of sin.

As Jesus ministered to the whole man, so must we, if we are true disciples of our Master. At home and abroad, as we minister to the physical needs of men in the name and in the spirit of Jesus, we shall often recognize that God has used us as instruments in his hand to bring them to recognize the King who has a right to reign in every heart.

5

Southern Baptists in World Evangelism

IN this day when orbiting satellites cut through space, when automation replaces the skilled worker, when electronics provide more and more of our home needs, when science offers escape from much physical suffering, it would seem that modern man might find a faster, more effective means of bringing release to hearts in bondage. But there is no short cut here.

"Whosoever shall call upon the name of the Lord shall be saved" (Rom. 10:13), said the apostle Paul, God's spokesman. But bringing individuals to the point of calling upon the Lord involves more, and again Paul describes the procedure: If men are to be saved, they must believe; and if they are to believe, they must hear the gospel; and if they are to hear the gospel, it must be preached; and if it is to be preached to the nations, there must be preachers; and if preachers (missionaries) go, they must be sent.

Human personality, then, offers the only medium

through which Christ's love can be communicated even in this "space age." Persons by the millions need to hear; persons—evangels—must proclaim; persons must send. God has, therefore, paid us the high compliment of responsibility for sharing his redemptive love in Christ. The eternal destiny of millions of souls depends upon it. He has granted to us this ministry of reconciliation.

"HOW SHALL THEY HEAR?"

The missionary has always been the heart of missions. All that we have read about in these pages has concerned dedicated persons. Without them there would be no story to tell.

Southern Baptists' first foreign missionary, Samuel C. Clopton, was commissioned September 1, 1845. He and George Pearcy, appointed later that year, sailed for China the following summer. When they were appointed, J. Lewis Shuck had been in China ten years already; he was appointed by the southern board in 1847 and assigned to Shanghai, with Matthew T. Yates and T. W. Tobey, who were appointed in 1846. Missionary Thomas J. Bowen went to Nigeria (1850), George B. Taylor to Italy (1873), John Westrup to Mexico (1880), Mr. and Mrs. William B. Bagby to Brazil (1881), the John W. McCollums and the John A. Brunsons to Japan (1889).

These were men and women of vision and faith. They and their colleagues laid a foundation of human devotion and service. Succeeding generations have built upon their work.

Through the first century of its history the Foreign Mission Board moved forward slowly. The world seemed larger then than now, and not many Southern Baptists could see beyond their local responsibilities. Wars, depressions, controversies, and limited concern were obstacles which slowed the forward pace. But God and events kept dealing with our world and with us.

At the end of the first century a grand total of 519 Southern Baptist missionaries were serving in fourteen countries. World War II was coming to a close. The whole world had changed, and our attitudes toward the world had undergone drastic revision. An increasing number of people, especially those who had served this country overseas, knew that we in the United States could never hide behind "our" oceans again. "Faraway places with strange-sounding names" became table conversation. Old concepts were shattered. Interested, open minds were ready for a bright challenge.

The challenge came from the late Dr. M. Theron Rankin in the spring of 1948 when, as executive secretary of the Foreign Mission Board, he called upon Southern Baptists to launch out with Christ in a program of advance in their worldwide witness. "Southern Baptists cannot continue," he said, "to answer the world call with six hundred missionaries and an average per capita gift of seventy cents a year."

Since that time, the number of missionaries under appointment for foreign service has doubled. The Board now has set a goal of eighteen hundred missionaries under appointment by January 1, 1964. This is a worthy challenge. It means that we must rise to new levels of life commitment.

There are many evidences that this dedication of life, leadership, and material goods is increasing. Developments in recent years point up the fact that more people are learning compassion for others who, being sick, have no physician; being hungry, have no one to feed them; being lost, have no one to tell them of a Saviour.

This high expectancy for real advance has not come overnight. It has come through persistent praying, patient planning, and the hard work of many servants of Christ at home and abroad.

Since the beginning of "Advance" eleven years ago, we have appointed 1,007 new missionaries, or an average of 90 per year. During that time we have lost 352 by retirement, death, and resignation. This is an average of 32 (about 3 per cent) lost per year.

In order to reach the goal of eighteen hundred in five years we must appoint an average of 155 missionaries each year. This will allow for the same percentage of losses, an estimate which seems realistic.

In setting goals for the appointment of new missionaries we do not emphasize numbers in any superficial way. It is because of the pressing need for far more missionaries that we respond to the urgency of the world situation. We have specific requests from mission countries for more than seven hundred new missionaries to be sent out as soon as possible.

"HOW SHALL THEY PREACH?"

"Make the most of your opportunity, for these are evil times," Goodspeed translates the apostle Paul's words in Ephesians 5:16. Young people all across our land are answering that call.

Well over half of the requests that come to the Board for missionary couples are for preachers and their wives. This is always true. No matter what else may be pointed up as an urgent, critical need, you may be assured that the most numerous and, therefore, the most urgent needs are for men who are called and trained to preach the gospel of a saving Christ, and for dedicated wives to stand by their sides. The day of the specialist is dawning, but the star of the general practitioner remains ever bright.

In a number of countries in which our missionaries work we do not have even one missionary for each one million people. Nine million Southern Baptists have more than 28,000 ordained preachers serving here in the homeland; about 450 preachers represent us in the name of Christ in all the rest of the world. Could this be God's intention? Did Christ go to the cross that only a favored minority of people should have every opportunity throughout life to hear the gospel, while most of the earth's people go from birth to death without ever hearing this good news? Everything in the New Testament answers with a resounding no!

Another area of opportunity that continues to call for strengthening is the field of religious education. Well-trained men are needed to teach in the seminaries. Others are needed to help publish literature for Sunday school, Training Union, and youth organizations. Still others face the challenge of promotional work among the young, growing churches. The Foreign Mission Board could use twenty couples in this type of service if they were available at this time.

An opportunity for student evangelism looms large before us. A recent study reveals some cities with as many as sixty thousand college students among whom no concerted evangelistic effort is being made by any evangelical group.

Groups of English-speaking people are banding together to form Baptist churches in many of the major cities of the world. Our Board has already answered calls from a few of them for leadership, but many other struggling groups are without pastors.

The whole field of academic education offers fertile ground for sowing seed of Christian witness. While the demands for missionary teachers at the secondary and elementary levels are not so numerous as they are at more advanced schools, they are, nonetheless, urgent. The colleges which our Board has helped develop need men and women of high academic attainment and warm Christian concern.

The greatest opportunities for teaching are to be found in our theological seminaries and institutes. The missionary teacher in any country has before him the need for indigenous churches. It is not enough to win people to a saving knowledge of Christ; those same people must be helped to organize themselves into New Testament churches that will carry on the task of evangelism. Unless leaders can be trained to "rightly divide the word of truth," there is no real hope for an indigenous church.

Medical missions has long held a vital spot in the heart of Southern Baptists. The stories told of bodies made whole and souls saved in the eighteen hospitals and sixty-two clinics and dispensaries on Southern Baptist mission fields are among the most thrilling of all. While additional doctors are continually requested, the need for missionary nurses is probably the most critical which the Board faces in its total personnel situation. The present ratio of fifty-five nurses to forty-six doctors reveals the urgent need.

For the past four years there have been repeated pleas for from twenty to thirty nurses to fill vacancies that already exist in Baptist medical institutions. Two mission hospitals have been in operation for more than eighteen months without a single missionary nurse.

In order to undertake even modest expansion of our program of medical evangelism, we should appoint fifty nurses during the next five years. Are Southern Baptists ready to draw the line on its great program of healing witness? If we continue as we are going, that alternative is inescapable.

There are also limited but definite opportunities in medical missions for technologists and hospital administrators.

Only single women can fill some positions in mission areas. In addition to serving as nurses and teachers, they find rich opportunities in such endeavors as Good Will Centers, Vacation Bible schools, and promotional work with Woman's Missionary Union organizations.

From time to time opportunities appear for missionaries trained in other fields of specialized ministry. There are needs for men skilled in the field of church music. There are a few openings in the vital area of agricultural missions. There are responsibilities for dedicated men trained in the business world and for young women who would serve as secretaries in mission headquarters offices.

DEDICATED TO WORLD SERVICE

Our prayer is that Southern Baptists may become increasingly aware of a lost world and of personal responsibility to God for doing something about it. That this very thing is happening is evident in the increasing number of young people committing their lives to God's leadership for overseas service. The testimony of Pat Carter, appointed recently for service in Mexico, gives evidence of this growing concern:

"I first began to restudy God's will for my life in the fall of 1955 when during Mission Day at Southwestern Seminary I felt that perhaps I had not settled the question of foreign mission service after all. In the years that followed that impression became dormant, and I decided once more that the question had been settled. However, in the fall of 1957, at another Mission Day service, I became absolutely convinced of the fact that God wanted me in foreign missions, and since that time this conviction has deepened continually. This call has been the most wonderful thing that has ever happened in my life.

"Accepting the call has necessitated a complete rethinking of what Christ meant when he gave the Great Commission. I came to see that it was not given with the idea that only a few people with a strange Damascus-road experience should go overseas to tell the bulk of humanity about Christ, but that the Great Commission includes everyone who is truly a Christian.

"I came to understand that with Christ there is no such thing as 'home missions' and 'foreign missions,' that there is only 'the world,' and that the attitude of every man called to preach must be, not, 'I'll serve in America unless God convinces me that I must serve overseas,' but rather, 'My call is to preach the gospel somewhere in God's world. Now, Lord, where is that to be?'

"When I came to that understanding of the call to missions and began to realize what a small group of people is trying to minister to the greater population in the lost world, I prayed, 'Lord, please call me for foreign mission service.' And he did! I am absolutely convinced that God has called me as a foreign missionary—as convinced as I am of my call to preach.

"The strange thing is that instead of looking upon the prospect of mission service as a sacrifice, I now look upon it as the most wonderful thing that has ever happened in my life. Where not long ago the thought of going as a missionary sent a chill of apprehension through me, I now would be desperately disappointed if I should not be able to go. This change, I know, was God's doing! I am also thankful that God has brought my wife to precisely the same deep conviction.

"As I think of leaving the country with my wife and three children, it is with the deepest sense of certainty that we go, led of God, and with the deepest and most profound gratitude that he has led us to see his perfect will for our lives."

Twelve thousand young men are preparing themselves to be Southern Baptist ministers and thousands of other young men and women are preparing for other professions that could be used effectively on the mission field. Within the next five years, as preparations are made for advance beyond 1964, we should have at least twice as many as we now have making preparation for some type of missionary service.

A significant trend in recent years is the large number of well-trained young pastors and their wives—in active, growing pastorates—who are offering themselves for missionary service. Choice laymen in the fields of business, education, and medicine are taking similar steps. This is one of the brightest hopes for immediate advance on many world frontiers.

Even in the face of urgent needs, the Foreign Mission Board has wisely held, and must continue to hold, high requirements for missionary appointment. The answer to the challenge of advance in personnel is not the lowering of standards. This would undermine the total mission undertaking within a few years.

When a missionary goes to a strange country, the combination of climate, language, culture, food, and other general living conditions to which he is unaccustomed has a way of conspiring to expose the weak spots in his personal armor. If he is not thoroughly equipped physically, emotionally, and spiritually, the chances are that he will be unable to render maximum service and that he will eventually be forced to return to the homeland. The Foreign Mission Board, under God's leadership, tries in every possible way to avoid this. It is encouraging to note that during recent years only one in eight persons given full consideration by the Board was advised to remain in America to serve Christ.

The need is for many more young people who will step forth to offer themselves for appointment. These young people must be dedicated to world service, wholehearted in commitment, clearheaded in purpose, realistic in self-appraisal, and persistent in preparation that is adequate for the challenge of the world's conflicting ideas. Only the best is worthy of Christ's usefulness.

It is not altogether easy to become a missionary. The road of preparation is usually long. Requirements are high, but not too high for the good, average young person who wants most of all to serve Christ in his appointed place. The wonder of the atmosphere of love, prayer, concern, and support with which Southern Baptists surround a missionary of this Board once he is appointed cannot be adequately described.

Two M.K.'s (missionary kids), one the son of Southern Baptist missionaries and the other of missionaries of another board, were talking about a particular situation they faced. Said the Southern Baptist M.K., "You just got born under the wrong Board!"

The Foreign Mission Board, the organizational framework by which Southern Baptists implement their purpose to witness effectively to the power of Christ in the world, is ever seeking new ways to present the claim of God on young lives for world service. There is a growing, contagious enthusiasm for personal participation in the mission task as other organizations in the Convention sound the note of advance. The Baptist Student Union, the Training Union, the Sunday school, Woman's Missionary Union, and Brotherhood are placing increasing emphasis upon the need for dedicated lives in world witness.

Missions conferences for college students are held annually on a number of the Baptist seminary campuses. Similar conferences for medical and nursing students have gained enthusiastic response. Youth rallies held in connection with associational Schools of Missions provide information and inspiration for many young people. Churches are finding ways to promote periodic fellowship meetings for young people who are seeking God's guidance regarding service overseas.

Every person who faces the possibility that God

may be calling him for foreign mission service is urged to write to the Department of Missionary Personnel of the Foreign Mission Board, Richmond, Virginia. Realizing that the writer's concern at this point does not in any way represent a lifetime commitment to the Foreign Mission Board, the personnel secretaries will send information about mission needs, types of service, requirements for appointment, and procedure toward appointment. Young people are encouraged to write even before they have come to any definite decision, in order that they may explore all possibilities related to God's leadership toward world witness.

"EXCEPT THEY BE SENT"

The Particular Baptist Society for Propagating the Gospel Among the Heathen was in business session. It was the year 1792.

After examining Dr. John Thomas' account of religious conditions among pagan peoples, Andrew Fuller remarked, "There is a gold mine in India, but it seems almost as deep as the center of the earth." Then he asked, "Who will venture to go down?"

William Carey instantly replied, "I will venture to go down, but," he looked at the men around him, "remember that you must hold the ropes."

Fuller's reply was reassuring: "This we solemnly engage to do and pledge ourselves never to desert you as long as we live." [1]

The congregation which Carey served as pastor

[1] *William Carey,* by John Brown Myers (Kilmarnock, Scotland: John Ritchie), p. 32.

was so reluctant to lose him that two members of the Baptist Society visited the church to pacify them. Perhaps one member spoke for the others when he said, "We have been praying for the spread of Christ's Kingdom amongst the heathen, and now God requires us to make the first sacrifice to accomplish it." [2]

These two incidents illustrate the whole missionary process. In response to the need of people in India, a missionary volunteered, a church gave one of its own (its pastor) to go, and a missionary society appointed him and promised to support him.

Back of all the significant events leading to the organization of the Baptist Missionary Society in England and to Carey's venture in India, are the factors that produce all missionary conviction and action.

The earlier portion of this chapter was given to a consideration of the missionaries who "go down into the earth." This portion will deal largely with the obligations and opportunities of those who "hold the ropes."

MISSIONS INITIATED

Missions did not begin with Carey, but with God. "Missions means the extensive realization of God's redemptive purpose in Christ by means of human messengers." [3] Missions have always been in God's plan. It was God who "so loved the world that he

[2] *Ibid.*, p. 33.

[3] William Owen Carver, *Missions in the Plan of the Ages* (New York: Fleming H. Revell Company, 1909), p. 11.

gave his only begotten Son, that whosoever believeth in him should not perish, but have everlasting life" (John 3:16). It was God who was "in Christ, reconciling the world unto himself" (2 Cor. 5:19).

The author of missions is God. Ever since Adam and Eve committed sin in the Garden of Eden and estranged themselves from God, he, out of a heart of love and concern for those he created in his own image, has been searching for man and planning his redemption.

The historical origin of missions can be found in the work, life, and commands of Jesus Christ. Jesus came to reveal the Father to the world. "The Word was made flesh, and dwelt among us, (and we beheld his glory, the glory as of the only begotten of the Father)" (John 1:14).

Jesus came to minister to those in need: "Even as the Son of man came not to be ministered unto, but to minister, and to give his life a ransom for many" (Matt. 20:28). By example and by principles, Christ laid the foundations for projecting the kingdom of God into the hearts of men everywhere.

Jesus established his church, trained disciples, and empowered and commissioned them to evangelize the world. Significantly, he said, "as my Father hath sent me, even so send I you" (John 20:21).

MISSIONARY RESPONSE

The disciples became missionaries—some to a larger degree than others. Through them the gospel was proclaimed to the Samaritans, to an Ethiopian, to Cornelius, and to the Greeks at Antioch (Acts

8-11). As their Lord commanded, they proclaimed the gospel in Jerusalem, in Judea, in Samaria, and beyond.

Paul, after his encounter with Jesus on the Damascus road, became a missionary—an apostle "born out of due season"—who counted not the cost nor was rebuffed by persecution, storm, nor any other difficulty in his efforts to evangelize the men of his day. He traversed most of the Graeco-Roman world, preaching the gospel, founding churches, and interpreting his Christ to men of every community that he touched.

In every generation since, there have been those disciples whose thoughts and actions were so motivated that they sought "first the kingdom of God and his righteousness."

In calling the roll of those who awakened a missionary consciousness, we always turn to William Carey, who inspired English Baptists to organize for missionary endeavor. It was the publication of his "Enquiry" in 1791 and the preaching of his convincing sermon, "Expect Great Things from God; Attempt Great Things for God," that led to the organization on October 2, 1792, of "The Particular Baptist Society for Propagating the Gospel Among the Heathen." Moreover, he so believed the answers he gave in the Missionary Enquiry—

1. we ought to be missionary
2. God approves missionary work
3. the world needs Christian missions
4. the difficulties can be overcome—

that he volunteered to go. And for forty-one years, without a furlough, he labored prodigiously and effectively in India.

Response also came from "great hearts" on the western side of the Atlantic. Two of God's noblest from a group of dedicated young men were Adoniram Judson and Luther Rice. As Congregationalist missionaries they sailed separately in 1812 for India, and on their way became convinced Baptists. They asked for baptism at the hands of Carey's colleague, William Ward, soon after their arrival in India.

Their seemingly tragic misfortune of being refused permission to remain in India was, we now believe, a part of God's wonderful providence. He used Rice in America and Judson in Burma to quicken the missionary consciousness among Baptists in America. Representatives of these aroused Baptists, desiring to "hold the ropes" for the Judsons in Burma and to discharge their missionary obligation made so plainly inescapable by Rice, met in Philadelphia in May, 1814. They organized the General Missionary Convention of the Baptist Denomination in the United States of America for Foreign Missions.

Although Judson and Rice were appointed missionaries of the Baptist convention immediately, Rice was asked to remain in the United States temporarily "to assist in originating societies or institutions for carrying the missionary design into execution." Another milestone in missionary response was reached when, for the first time in America, Baptists began to co-operate in the mission task.

Another singular development toward missionary response was the organization of the Southern Baptist Convention in 1845. Recognizing their obligation to evangelize the homeland, delegates to this Convention at its constituting meeting created a Domestic Board (now the Home Mission Board). But keeping in mind their responsibility to proclaim the gospel beyond the boundaries of the nation, the newly organized Southern Baptist Convention set up a board for foreign missions.

Since its creation, the Foreign Mission Board has been the channel through which Southern Baptists have sent missionaries "deep" into the world and through which they have "held the ropes" with their prayers, money, abiding concern, and support.

Through these 114 years Southern Baptists have given 2,441 of their sons and daughters to foreign mission service. (Significantly enough, more than half of them are in active service now.) Moreover, they have placed on the altar $195,052,403.91 to strengthen and hold fast the ropes that their noble ambassadors might bear witness of God's redeeming grace to the peoples who "walked in darkness."

NEED ABOUNDS

Let us come to the present. Our forefathers bore their burdens and shouldered many responsibilities for the kingdom of Christ, and we honor them for their achievements in missions. But Southern Baptists, as well as all other Christian groups, face a world of tremendous need. They must not fail to discharge their responsibility to bring into operation all their abilities, devotion, and means to alleviate this need.

Surely, ours is a world in need. Probably the very word "need" in all its forms and implications more nearly characterizes the peoples of the world than any other word.

The world is in need of food, shelter, and clothing. Refugees from Communist China continue to pour into Hong Kong and Macao, where, but for quick relief, they would succumb to hunger and disease. In Korea, thousands are destitute because of the results of a war which, though nearly five years past, continues to make life exceedingly difficult and a livelihood hard to come by. Arab refugee camps continue to dot the hills of Lebanon, Syria, Jordan, and the Gaza Strip.

We in America live on an island of plenty that is afloat in a world of want, misery, and physical need. Surely, John included us when he wrote, "But whoso hath the world's goods, and beholdeth his brother in need, and shutteth up his compassion from him, how doth the love of God abide in him?" (1 John 3:17 ASV).

The world is also in need of Christian schooling. The nine hundred Baptist schools in our mission areas are not able to accept the number of students who would like to attend. They are crowded with the 129,800 students who are enrolled now. Some missionaries report that twenty-five schools for every school now on their fields would not meet the present demand.

The Foreign Mission Board has urgent requests

for many educational missionaries to teach in the academic schools already in existence on the several mission fields. When we realize that boys and girls whom we could never reach otherwise come to our academic schools, and that many of them become Christians and later outstanding denominational leaders, we are confronted with the strategic importance of meeting the need for schools.

Moreover, we must strengthen the theological schools we now have, and build others. Without them, it is not possible to have a trained national ministry to evangelize the peoples who live in the thirty-eight countries where Southern Baptists missionaries now serve.

The world also stands in need of medical care. More than a billion of the earth's people lack medical care of one kind or another, and will not be able to get it. In Indonesia, for example, there is only one doctor for every fifty thousand people and only one nurse for every hundred thousand. Southern Baptists have one hospital in that land, but many more could not begin to meet the need for hospitals throughout the country.

Our eighteen hospitals and sixty-two dispensaries and clinics on foreign fields, together with those of other sponsoring agencies, are like oases sprinkled through a vast desert. But people who are ill cannot always travel great distances, and even if they could they would find the hospital overcrowded.

Above all, the world is in need of salvation. Most of the approximately 2,800,000,000 souls who people the earth do not know the Lord Christ in personal faith. These "lost" souls in our homeland number into the millions; in foreign lands they number nearly 2,000,000,000.

In Asia, where the total population is about 1,600,000,000, less than 45,000,000, or 2.8 per cent, are Christians. In Africa, only 35,000,000 of a population numbering some 225,000,000 are Christians. Of the 43,000,000 increase in the world's population last year, only 10,500,000 were claimed by any Christian group as believers, and these included all the Catholics numbered.

"The more we learn of the history of the human race, through the long, slow-moving millenniums of ignorance, superstition, struggle, strife, futile groping," the late Dr. W. O. Carver once said, "the more emphatic becomes the demonstration of their need of God; and the need for a Redeemer to give new outlook, new spiritual energy, and a new urge in achieving the very meaning of humanity." [4]

The apostle Paul pictures the tragedy of human depravity, perversity, and personal and social sin. And as a remedy for all of this, he everywhere lifts up the cross of Calvary, which bears the infinite personal love of God in the redeeming Christ who loved men and gave himself for them.

People all over the world lack food, Christian education, medicine, and salvation. These needs demand that we exert our utmost in an honest attempt to meet them.

[4] *The Furtherance of the Gospel* (Nashville: The Sunday School Board, 1935), p. 47.

OUR RESOURCES

The resources of Southern Baptists put us under an everlasting obligation to be more missionary. First of all, we have the young people God needs as missionaries. Surely, God has called from among Southern Baptist young people enough missionaries to meet the urgent requests from the mission fields for 742 additional missionaries who are needed now. Every church has a remarkable opportunity to cultivate the young people of its membership whom God may call into foreign mission service. The cutting edge of foreign missions is the missionary, and without the missionary, foreign missions becomes an impossibility.

The nerve center of any worthwhile movement of expanded Christian witness is the church and its pastor. It has been conservatively estimated that of all the missionaries on the field today, at least 80 per cent had their first impressions for world service in the home church. There is a mass of evidence to verify this conclusion.

As missionary candidates come before the Foreign Mission Board to give personal testimonies, such words as these are heard: "God used Royal Ambassadors as a vehicle to bring my call to foreign mission service"; or, "My Sunday school teacher, by leading us to pray for specific missionaries each Sunday morning, caused me to take missions seriously"; or again, "My pastor had wanted to go to the field but could not meet the requirements. He always kept before us the command of Christ and the needs of lost people."

As members of each church face the opportunity for doing something personally about world witness and pray for God to call out their finest young people, we will see a miracle take place. In fact, it has already begun. Hardly a day passes but that some pastor writes to tell about the decision of a young person who has offered his life in full commitment to Christ.

Southern Baptists have the young people God needs as missionaries, and they also have the money our Lord expects them to give for missions. Last year the income of our church members totaled approximately $17,000,000,000. A tithe of that would be $1,700,000,000, but we did not give the tithe. We gave only $419,619,438 for all causes. This was only about 2½ per cent of our income and about one fourth of our tithes.

Of our total gifts of $419,619,438, we Southern Baptists gave only $74,750,699 for all missions. This means that $344,868,739, or 82.3 per cent, was used by the churches to meet local expenses and undertakings; only 17.7 per cent was left for all the demands of Southern Baptist work beyond that of the churches' local programs.

Take a look at the "foreign missions" portion of the money given for missions. Of the total amount, $15,340,246, or 3.6 per cent, represents in dollars the concern of Southern Baptists for the lost souls in the part of the world beyond our country. Can we boast of our individual interest in foreign missions when we find that each Southern Baptist averaged giving $1.67 for missions overseas?

Then again, we have unhindered access to God through prayer. If Southern Baptists would give themselves to fervent and continuous prayer for missions, the achievements around the world would exceed our highest imaginations. Do we not believe that "the effectual fervent prayer of a righteous man availeth much" (James 5:16)?

Half, or even a fourth, of the nine million Southern Baptists constitute prayer power that could remove mountains. If one fourth of the members in our churches would pray fervently for missions, they would bring all of us so close to God we could not but say, "What may I do to help send a missionary to yonder lands?" Our Lord has promised, "If ye shall ask anything in my name, I will do it" (John 14:14). Let us fall upon our knees and pray, and arise to our feet to claim that promise in faithful conquest.

Since we Southern Baptists have all the resources in personnel, money, and prayer to do what God expects of us, there seems to be no excuse for failure to discharge our full stewardship responsibility. Let us pray earnestly for the development of a genuine missionary passion and zeal. A fresh appraisal of our obligation surely would leave all of us with the realization that we ought to be missionary.

This responsibility is ours because Jesus commanded it. Did he not say, "Go ye therefore, and make disciples of all the nations" (Matt. 28:19 ASV)? The inescapable obligation his command places upon all of us who are his is that we, by our witness, bring all men to believe upon him.

Moreover, we ought to be missionary because we are empowered to be. Jesus' last words to his disciples before his ascension constitute a promise of great significance: "But ye shall receive power, after that the Holy Ghost is come upon you" (Acts 1:8). The words of the promise convey also the purpose for which that power is bestowed.

We are impelled to be missionary, and that which impels us is love. Jesus gave us the best statement we have on the principle of love: "If ye love me, keep my commandments" (John 14:15). The commandment is plain; the promise of power for the task is definite. Yet, many of us have failed to be missionary in any enterprising fashion. Could it be that our love for our Lord is too little?

Writing in the June, 1951, issue of *The Commission,* Dr. M. Theron Rankin said, "Most important of all is the crucial question: What *will* we say to God? He knows all about us. Answer him we must. It is not a question of what *would* we say, but what *will* we say. Will we say, 'Lord, we couldn't do so much for the world and do the other things we wanted to do also'?

"But what are the other things we want to do and which we put first? We have all kinds of explanations which we can give to one another, but will they stand up when we give them to God? Suppose you try. I have and it won't work. I can only say, 'Lord, forgive us; forgive us, O, God.'

"What will *you* say?"